Reclaim Your Heart Power

How to Heal Your Heart and Find Personal Power After Narcissistic Abuse

Jennifer Licciardi

Cover designed by Robert Maynard

Jennifer Licciardi
Visit my website at www.reclaimheartpower.com

Printed in the United States of America

First Printing: September 2023
Amazon/KDP

ISBN-13 979-8-218-28129-8

CONTENTS

Acknowledgements

I have learned to see everyone who has entered my life as a spiritual teacher or gift. Each of you has provided me with the lessons needed to grow, which prepared me to step into my life purpose or calling. I'm grateful for all the tears, anger, and heartache because it was needed, designed to help me learn, grow, and expand my soul, so that I can help other women.

Thank you, God, for always loving, protecting, and guiding me.

Thank you supporting me every moment of the day.

I'm grateful that You are holding my hand, and for all of Your preparation that gave me the strength to walk forward into my purpose, or calling.

I want to thank all of the women who are reading my book. I truly wish for you to love yourself fully, heal your heart, find your voice, step into your personal power, having discovered your heart power within. I'm so blessed to be a part of your journey as you join me on mine.

I want to extend a special thank you to Olivia Marshall Photography for perfectly capturing my energy for the cover photo of this book.

I want to give a special thanks to my relationship coaches who pushed me to get out of my comfort zone, teaching me that I'm the only one who can change my life. They were able to show me the steps, but I was the one who had to take them.

I want to thank my parents for always being supportive and believing in me. You taught me that I can achieve anything I set my mind to. I'm incredibly grateful for the double dose of drive and self-motivation you gave me.

I want to say thank you to my amazing manager.

He was so supportive during my Spiritual Awakening. I'm eternally grateful that you showed me how to be centered, calm, and find peace in my life no matter what is happening externally.

Introduction

Your life's journey is an exquisite adventure, leading you back to the wellspring of your own love—a force capable of unshackling you from life's constraints and igniting the power within. This love is your sacred compass, your guiding star on the path of healing, heart expansion, and self-empowerment. I warmly invite you to join me on this extraordinary journey where I candidly share the steps that have carried me from being a relentless people-pleaser, hungering for external approval, to a woman who proudly embodies her personal power, forging a life of fulfillment.

As I recount my own remarkable transformation, you'll discover the profound shifts that reshaped my world, unveiling the blessings that have eternally resided within my heart. This voyage is not just about storytelling; it's a transformational guide, a roadmap of the precise steps that have led to my extraordinary metamorphosis.

I'm offering you crystal-clear guidance on how to infuse these practices into your own life, and, at the end of each section, you'll find reflection questions and actions to help you navigate this path alongside me.

Are you prepared to embark on the quest of unearthing the masterpiece concealed beneath the layers of outdated narratives and societal conditioning?

Together, we shall embark on this sacred journey of awakening your heart's intrinsic power, empowering you to confidently step into your personal authority and craft the life your heart has always yearned for.

It All Starts with You

"A woman is the full circle. Within her is the power to create, nurture, and transform."
—Diane Mariechild

If you take one key message from this book, I hope that message is… Are you ready for it?

It all starts with you.

Everything you need is already inside of you. When you realize this truth, it is such a powerful moment or at least it was for me.

What does that even mean?

When I first heard these words of wisdom, I asked myself that very question. It means that you have everything you need to open your heart, to heal, to find your voice, to create an entirely new life already inside of you.

How is that even possible?

You are probably thinking, *"If I have everything I already need, then why am I struggling, why am I stuck, and why did I buy this book?"*

I'm going to bring you along on my journey to show you how I discovered that it all starts with you, and that I already had the power within to change my entire world in every way. Wow! Let that sink in for a moment. I'm going to say every one of you has the ability to tap into the power within you.

How do you find that power inside of you?

First and foremost, it takes having an open mind and getting out of your comfort zone.

You will begin to find that power by trying a new approach.

Do you want to meet this work of art underneath your past beliefs and old stories you have told yourself? It's time to come face to face with the true you who has been there all along, hidden behind all the masks you wear.

Isn't it time to meet her, and give her a voice?

This won't be an easy journey, but I can tell you it is one that will truly be worth it.

Walking through the parts of you that you have kept hidden, buried deep down, that you almost forgot are still there will take some bravery.

It is your destiny to meet **all** of you…

Your birthright as a woman is to find your true essence within….

If you are reading this book, you most likely have something inside saying that there is more to life. You are tired of feeling stuck, in the status quo, and/or living an unfulfilled life.

If you choose to, this can be the day that all of that begins to change for you.

The day you begin to reclaim your heart power, taking it back….

Your own love will heal your heart.

So many of you have searched for love in a romantic relationship. I have been guilty of this many times. One of my life changing moments was over a decade ago when I realized that loving myself, that little girl within me, would forever change my world. I loved myself to heal trauma, which I'll share more of later in this book.

The power is within your heart and always has been. You just didn't know it. The more you love yourself, the better all of your relationships will become in all aspects of your life. Most importantly, the better your relationship will become with you.

Why Is It Important to Heal?

Choose to heal for you and for everyone in your life.

Show girls and/or women in your life that they are worth it.

Be that role model and end that generational trauma with you.

Show them that they can be and do anything, completely changing their lives for the better by healing within.

When you heal, you will be able to manage triggers quickly and more effectively, and be triggered far less often.

Over the years, I've done a lot of healing work. Much of my journey to become a coach myself has involved working with relationship coaches.

When I get triggered now, I say thank you. I see it as an opportunity to release what needs to come to the surface to be healed. I sit with those feelings as they come up, feeling those emotions bubble to the surface. Then I picture those feelings/emotions leaving my body.

I see them float by in clouds or bubbles right by me.

I find visualizations to be very powerful, and I use them in my coaching. Healing isn't linear, so there is always more healing work to do throughout your life. It's about learning how to heal so much is ready to be released.

Personal experience has taught me that it may feel scary to open your heart even to yourself.

Having been in a number of narcissistic relationships throughout my life, I didn't let anyone in, even myself.

I didn't want to feel bad any more or ever again.

I didn't want to feel judged, hurt, belittled, or go back to feeling or reliving that trauma.

For a long time, I didn't trust myself.

I thought choosing bad relationships was my fault. I clearly did not have a good radar system, having been in more than one narcissist relationship.

A decade ago, I didn't even know that term. I called it an unhealthy or emotionally abusive relationship. I knew it was unhealthy because he was controlling, condescending, and I was always walking on eggshells. Everything I read now screams in all the worst possible ways that I was with a full- blown narcissist. I read a post showing signs of a narcissist and he would meet practically all of them.

Heal to Know What a Healthy Relationship Looks Like

It's time to heal so that you know what a healthy relationship looks like, and not repeat the pattern of bringing another narcissist into your life.

They slip in so easily and then, all of a sudden, you ask, *"How did I get here again?"* Sometimes one enters your life and it's the person you least expected to be one. A narcissist will groom you little by little, so it's imperative that you see through their game before you get too invested. There are a number of different types of narcissists.

and I want to spend some time in this first chapter getting clear on narcissistic behavior so that you see the small flags really early on.

Six Tactics of a Narcissist

1. **Love Bombing**. A narcissist wants you to feel amazing. They make you think that you have finally found the one and that you are meant to be together. They shower you with attention and affection. You can do no wrong. They say how

8

amazing you are, how much they adore you, and love everything about you.

Anyone who comes on this strong is insecure. The narcissist will exude confidence often, but typically it is for show. He needs to rope you in quickly so that you will think the world of him, and do anything to have his back.

What can you do to figure out if you are being love bombed by a narcissist?

- **Don't drop everything in your day to take every call or text**. This isn't a game that you are playing.
- **Don't be all in so quickly**. Get to know this person little by little. If you aren't playing his game, he will get upset with you, or back away himself because he realizes that you aren't a good mark.
- **Don't hang on every word**. You can show a healthy interest in someone without being at his beck and call.
- **Create healthy, loving boundaries**. Still make time for your friends and other activities. When you are out with others, don't respond to all his texts about how he can't stop thinking about you and how much he misses you. A healthy relationship will require balance, and a secure man will not need to check on you all the time.
2. **Shares Everything.** The narcissist will open up to you, sharing a lot of personal stuff about his life. This is where he may be emotional while opening up to you, and may even cry in front of you on occasion. He is more sensitive, letting you into some of his personal, inner world of how he is feeling. He wants to run his ideas by you for approval so

that he feels good knowing that you are there cheering him on.

This one really threw me.

My ex-boyfriend, "Greg", and I were in a long- term relationship. I believed him to be a narcissist who was very closed off emotionally. He had a hard time opening up and sharing anything really personal, including his feelings.

I hate to admit it, but I briefly dated two men who I would consider to be narcissists. I thought it was healthy to see a man I was getting to know be vulnerable with me and cry. Be aware of this type of narcissist because, as in my experience, they can be very confusing.

3.   **Controlling Behavior.** When a narcissist is controlling, he wants to call all the shots. It can be subtle at first because he is making the plans, being what you may call "the man" in a relationship. He may have strong opinions on what you do and who you choose to spend your time around. He wants to be the focus and center of your world, always coming first.

Over time, it became clear to me.

I was told what clothes to wear, who to spend time with, how to wear my hair, or I should be smiling more.

There was even a certain way I needed to cook and clean. To him, I was being too much like Eeyore, so that was my new nickname.

The early signs are sometimes hard to spot. Early on, everything was on his schedule, and I didn't even notice it. I loved spending time in San Francisco where he lived, so I would gladly drive the two hours to get there. Being in outside sales, I had a more flexible work schedule, so I wasn't tied to an office. I worked from home and visited customers.

I was making more of an effort early on.

This made everything convenient for him.

I didn't even notice at the time. He kept planning fun things for us to do that were mostly where he lived. There was also this push-pull that happened where he was wanting to spend time with me versus his new friends. He was the one in control really from the beginning. It was all done so subtly. Looking back, I realized that he was trying to figure out life after his divorce. His wife left him, and I didn't know that she had rushed the divorce. He never spoke badly of her. Instead, he just said that it didn't work out. They were two bigger personalities who butted heads often. He always bragged about how he put her through med school by paying the bills, and that she left him when she became a doctor.

4.   **All About Him.** The narcissist will find a way to make things all about him. He will always want and need your support even early on. He may use you as a sounding board for all his decisions, wanting to run everything by you first. He really wants to feel your light and positive energy, which is all about feeding his needs. He wants to hear that you love his idea, that he's brilliant, that you are so proud of him– all feeding his ego.

The last time I was with a narcissist, I needed support.

It didn't happen often, but he would act like he was there for me, yet it felt off. Since then, I've gotten myself to a healthy point of having strong self-love and self-worth. I can feel when someone isn't really there for me.

When I was sharing, I didn't feel true empathy or a connection. He seemed bothered that I wasn't shining my light and radiating that positive energy that he could feed off of.

I would say to myself, "I'm not feeling loving support." It felt more like he was going through the motions.

Pay attention to how you feel during your interactions with a narcissist. In the beginning phases, it's easy to ignore the signs because they can be so subtle.

I was curious, wanting to know more about his past, his marriage, why they really got divorced, and the timeframe when the divorce was finalized. He was officially divorced when we met, but I was too afraid to ask these questions, and I don't know why. I truly believe the key to seeing who someone really is underneath the masks they wear is by asking questions and really getting to know someone.

You have to watch by letting their behavior play out without getting sucked in.

During the first year, there were so many good times that it was easy enough to let go of the bad times.

I had invested so much time and energy that I just kept going. I knew relationships weren't supposed to be perfect, so I took this to be part of life.

5. **In the Spotlight.** The narcissist always has to be in the spotlight. It always has to be about him. If you begin to shine, then he will knock you down a peg or two, putting you in your place. He may say that you are getting full of yourself or that you need to be humbled. At first, the narcissist will gaslight you with love bombing, making this a tough one to notice. You can test if you are dealing with a narcissist by sharing your accomplishments and wins and watching how he reacts. Is he supportive, genuinely cheering you on or does he turn the conversation back to him? If he refocuses your conversation back to him, and

doesn't allow you to shine, then he most likely is a narcissist. This is an unhealthy relationship that isn't going to lift you up where you deserve to be. You were meant to shine, and the right man will be proud to hold your hand while you shine bright for all to see.

In my case, as I was becoming more confident, he wanted to knock me down a couple of pegs. I remember when I won President's Club, an award for the top performing sales reps in the country, I recall him saying, *"Congratulations sweetie! It's so nice that you can win without working very hard."* This was a big wake up call for me! I realized that, no matter what I did or accomplished, he was never going to let me shine. He was never going to support me or give credit as to how hard I worked to win. All the long hours in the hospital constantly following up with customers did not matter to him. He always had to be in the spotlight.

6. **Makes You Question Your Beliefs**. Narcissists have the ability to make you question yourself and your beliefs. There is a way the narcissist turns things around so that you become confused and somehow become more dependent on him.

I went through this fairly recently.

I believed this man to be a God driven connection as a lesson, a reminder, or test to see what I have learned. He was the last person I ever expected to be a narcissist.

I fell quickly as he opened up, sharing several personal life moments with me. He was attentive, said how much he adored me, and that he was so proud of me for all the big changes I made in my life. Most importantly, we also had a close connection to God. I was hopeful that this was the love that I had been so patiently waiting for.

To my surprise, he pushed and kept prodding, which caused me to question my beliefs that I held so strongly. He wanted to know where the proof was and asked how I knew things to be true. I even started questioning myself when he asked how I had the right to be a coach when I was still an emotional mess.

At that moment, I questioned all of it. I couldn't see or think straight. Even with all that I knew, I found myself tumbling down the rabbit hole.

Being an Empath, I couldn't tell whether I was picking up on his energy or mine.

I didn't know whose feelings were triggering me.

This painful experience was such a gift as it helped me to heal deep parts that I had buried.

Ones that I didn't even know existed any more....

At the same time, my heart ached as all my hopes and expectations came to an end with this connection. This turned out to be a valuable lesson, which allowed me to reconnect with that wounded part of me.

Doing so meant that I could connect with women even more as I wrote my book.

God did share that this man would be the one to help me rise to where He wants me to be. That happened in a very unexpected way I did not see coming. This experience is what allowed me to move directly into my soul mission or calling – helping women heal their hearts after narcissistic abuse.

The more inner healing work you do, the safer you will feel within your own body. The more you learn to trust yourself and the guidance you are receiving, the easier it will be to open your heart to the right person.

Heal to the point where you shine your light so brightly that the narcissist can't even find a way in!

Reflection Questions and Actions:

1. Check off which of the six tactics you've experienced. Then add them up as well to see how many of these tactics you've dealt with before. Feel free to add any that aren't here.

   Six Tactics:

   ____ Love Bombing

   ____ Shares Everything

   ____ Controlling Behavior

   ____ All About Him

   ____ In the Spotlight

   ____ Makes You Question Your Beliefs

2. How often did you feel bad about yourself, unloved, and unworthy in the relationship?

   ____ 1-3 times a month

   ____ 4-6 times a month

   ____ more than 6 times a month

   ____ Never

   ____ Sometimes

   ____ Often

   ____ Almost Always

3. What did you tell yourself that caused you to stay?

4. What was it that finally got you out of the narcissistic relationship?

5. Make a list of these signs and tactics for you to hold on to making sure to add any that I may have missed.

6. What do you want to learn from this book?

7. How will you stay motivated to do the necessary inner healing work? You can attract healthy relationships in all aspects of your life, including one with you.

The Five Pillars of Love

"BEING VULNERABLE is hard, but I've learned that sharing our true, flawed, authentic selves is the only way real connection and love can happen. It's the only way to step into our full power and purpose in our lives.
—Jamie Kern Lima

How Do You Get Started to Reclaim Your Heart Power?

In this chapter, I'm going to walk you through the steps I took to connect to my heart, find the love within me, and ultimately reclaim my heart power. In my healing journey, I have found that there are five key elements that were instrumental to lead me back to reclaim my heart power. I call them the Five Pillars of Love.

Pillar One: Gratitude or Appreciation.

When you begin to focus on what you already have, and are truly grateful for it, you will receive more of what's already thriving in your life. Part of this comes from you getting more of what you focus your energy on.

For example, if you think, *"I'm alone. There aren't any good men out there, and certainly not where I live."* Well, what do you get? I can tell you that God and the Universe will give you a matching frequency for what you are putting out there. In other words, you will be given exactly what you are asking for.

The Universe doesn't hear the word "don't", so you will be able to prove your point that there isn't anyone out there for you. In turn, that becomes a story that you tell yourself, which then turns into a limiting belief.

Instead, change that thought to, *"I know there are good men out there and, when the moment is right, I'm going to meet the right one for me."* Ask God to prepare you for your right person. Know that typically means growing you and big life changes as well.

The only way you grow to get what you truly desire in life, and to claim your destiny, is to get out of your comfort zone.

Every morning, I wake up and I say, "Thank you God for this amazing day. I'm so grateful for this amazing day." I set the intention that it is going to be an amazing day. I choose to focus on all the good things that happen, and I also choose to learn from anything not so good that happens. It's so important to find a blessing in each experience, and sometimes you may have to look a little harder, but one can typically be found. It's important not to dwell or fixate on anything that happened that day that may frustrate you. Again, feel your feelings, but don't stay stuck in that negative energy.

Why I shifted to a Gratitude Mindset

I was not living this way for a long time. I used to focus on what was missing. I was content with what I had, but not truly grateful. I find that there is a big difference.

What was it that happened to cause me to make such a huge change in my philosophy of life? A close friend of mine lost her husband in a car accident. They were both thirty- two years old and were high school sweethearts. She was left to raise a one-year-old and a three-year old. I saw how she held onto her faith through her tragic loss. What truly amazed me was that, shortly after he passed, she still found gratitude in her life. She was grateful for her kids, the beautiful sunset, and the family and friends who supported her.

I then changed my entire outlook to one of gratitude.

Shortly after his passing, she gave me a gratitude journal as a gift for my fortieth birthday. It was life changing.

I began to share what I was grateful for with everyone.

At the time, I was a medical sales rep, selling to hospitals, working in project management, and a field sales trainer.

The sales industry is looked at as very cyclical, and salespeople often have the nature of feeding off of each other's energy.

As I heard reps complain, I would say, *"Let's focus on the positive here. I just can't complain anymore about these insignificant things. My friend lost her husband in a car accident, is now raising her one-, and three-year-old children, and she still finds gratitude each day. If she can find gratitude, focusing on so much good, even with all that pain, then why can't we?"*

Looking back, this was the beginning of my lifting others up, and seeing the light within me shine through.

Reflection Questions and Actions:

1. How can I show more gratitude each day?
2. What am I truly grateful for? List all that is working in your life now. Get excited about what is thriving!
3. Create a daily gratitude practice and set that intention.

Pillar Two: Transparency or Vulnerability.

Take whichever word resonates more with you.

I wasn't exposed to either until I was thirty-four years old. Before now, I didn't use any of this language.

Social media wasn't what it is nowadays.

Self-improvement or growth language was kept pretty hidden back then.

Why is it so important to be vulnerable?

Being vulnerable or transparent allows you to get out of your comfort zone. The further you get outside of your comfort zone, the more you will grow. You stay stuck by repeating the same patterns, reliving old stories, and doing what feels safe and familiar.

Learn to feel your spirit, or soul, and not the ego. The ego's job is to keep you safe. Spirit or your soul's job is to connect you with the true essence of why you are here. It's all about bringing you home to who you truly are under all the old conditioning, outdated stories, and past beliefs.

When you are vulnerable or transparent, the real you will shine through. You take off the mask of who you show to the world, allowing for a deeper connection with those around you, and more importantly yourself.

Know that it is okay to be confused as to who you are in this process. This is a process of unbecoming who you thought you were all these years, who the outside world labeled you as, and what you have always thought or known to be true.

The answers you so desperately want are all inside of you. It's just a matter of connecting with that woman deep within you who wants to be a part of your daily life. You may hear her from time to time and not answer her pleas to connect with that beautiful, amazing, feminine, and magical part of you.

The magic will enter once you decide that you are ready to let her into your world. This is when life will make much more sense.

This will be the moment you realize that you had the power within you all along to change your current reality or the life you helped to create.

I've found vulnerability and transparency to come from the heart. When you are willing to speak from your heart when sharing with others, it is very healing. When it came to social media. I always kept to myself. If you look at my social media presence and the type of posts I put up before 2022, you would have little to no idea who I was.

Early in 2022, God/Spirit guided me to start sharing very personal, vulnerable posts all about my life on my personal Facebook page.

After going through my Spiritual Awakening, I knew that I was supposed to share my heart with the world. I had already been getting some practice sharing my personal life with both my relationship group and coach. I also spent several hours a day in Gabby Bernstein's Miracle Membership Group. There, I was sharing personal stories in posts and in the comments with over twelve thousand people around the world.

This was a whole different ball game. I knew that I was walking towards my calling by taking these steps very early in my Awakening, I saw myself writing books, speaking on stage professionally. In my heart, I knew these were my steppingstones to get to that new identity.

To my surprise, my personal stories were well received. I poured my heart out, opening up about heartbreak, being a people pleaser, being a workaholic, professional burnout, healing my inner child, getting out of my comfort zone, growing my self -love, how I found my faith, and the story of my Spiritual Awakening.

I continued to open up to everyone I came across.

I grew so much from being vulnerable or transparent and so can you. Start to think of areas that you've been vulnerable or transparent in your past and how those experiences have grown you and/or made you stronger. You are given opportunities to get out of the familiar and what you are comfortable with every day. It's up to you to decide whether or not to take them.

Reflection Questions and Actions:

1. How can I be more vulnerable or transparent each day?
2. Go up to a stranger or someone you know and share something with them that's genuine. It can be brief. Let people in. There are so many good people out there, and that's who you will attract in all areas of your life when you open up more. You need to be on the same frequency with these open, caring people. So often, you attract people who want to stay in their comfort zone, blend in, and live in fear of being seen.
3. Ask a question at work or share an idea you have.
4. Ask to make a plan to go out with friends. Take the lead. Go where you want to go, and don't think about what others may want. Put yourself out there being transparent, and own your decision no matter the outcome. Say to your colleagues, *"I think it would be fun to try someplace new."*
5. Get into new energy each day and out of the safety of the familiar by being vulnerable enough to try new things or new places.

Pillar Three: Inner Work or Healing.

This is where it all starts.

Much of your journey involves doing inner work, healing, growing, and preparing yourself to walk right into your destiny.

Healing means releasing old trauma that is keeping you stuck from moving forward, preventing you from loving yourself and feeling worthy, and connecting with who you really are deep within.

Healing is what will allow you to reclaim your heart power. Healing work helps you to realize that you are a whole, beautiful soul inside and out. You are here to heal and grow into who you are meant to be. The inner work you do will bring you back to who you truly are, letting go of all these parts that no longer resonate as you find your true self.

Healing and growing go hand in hand. One can't exist without the other. Healing may sound scary, not fun, and a lot of work. It's normal to question if you even have time for this right now. In reality, it is 100 percent necessary to create a healthy relationship with yourself and others.

Healing can help to improve your marriage as well as your relationship with your children, family, friends, and work colleagues.

Be a role model by showing that you are worth it, so others can learn from you.

My healing work began in late 2012 when I was blessed to have a new friend enter my life.

I met her at a friend's party and she wanted us all to be open and share our fears and the things on our mind that we didn't like to talk about. These were not topics that I was comfortable sharing in a room full of women, many who I didn't know.

This woman introduced herself as a relationship or love coach. She was adamant about working with me, saying she could help me. Somehow, I knew that I was supposed to work with her. At first, working with a coach didn't make any sense to me. I hadn't worked with a coach like this before.

When I was twenty-six years old, I worked with a therapist to learn how to feel my feelings and deal with some unhealthy codependency issues I had. I found that to be incredibly beneficial, so I said, "Okay. I will work with you when I feel ready."

I was building my life back up on the outside first, and feeling good about what I was creating. I had never created a life of my own before. This was my reality and I could make it anything that I wanted. I had work, a few close friends, and alone time.

I asked the coach for more time because I was still putting my life back together, but the truth was that I didn't want to face all that I experienced. I needed to become stronger first.

I joined the Women's Junior League with a friend of mine and a Women's Thirty Something Group on Meetup. I stayed super busy between work and my social life with so many amazing women, some who I am still friends with today.

For the first time in my life, I was now calling the shots. It was all about what I wanted to do, and what made me feel good.

Looking back, this was the beginning of rebuilding my self-confidence.

As you heal, you clear out old programming or conditioning.

You get rid of previous patterns, outdated stories, and past beliefs.

I'll go much more in depth in this area further in this book.

You will understand how logical this spiritual journey of growth and walking into your destiny really is.

The reason you're here and the meaning of your life will begin to make sense.

Healing allows you to connect fully with your own heart as you claim your heart power.

Healing grows your self-love and self-worth, builds your confidence, and helps you to feel more fulfilled.

Healing is the most powerful experience you can give yourself. It is a gift that you and others benefit from the rest of your life. Your healing will inspire other women to start their healing journey.

You will show all those around you that you were worth the work, you found your voice, and now stand in your highest personal power, sharing all of you with the world as God intended.

You are responsible for your own healing.

Start with the less traumatic experiences or what is showing up.

When you are triggered, see it as an opportunity.

This is a chance to heal what is coming up for you.

I will go a lot deeper into inner healing work further in this book.

While on a hike with a group of women, one of them opened up to me, sharing her life story. I saw her again on the next hike.

This time, I was excited to see her again.

I thought we would pick up where we left off. Instead, she told me she wanted to catch up with a friend she hadn't seen in a while.

She said, "We want to catch up, so you can go walk with the other two women."

For a moment, I was back to being that twelve-year-old girl in school who was told she couldn't sit at the lunch table. For a minute, I felt my eyes well up with tears as I ran to catch up to the other two ladies.

I told myself. *"You are not that child anymore. You are a goddess, a strong, confident woman, who has grown so much."*

Just like that, I shifted my perspective and smiled, honoring that child because she helped me become who I am today.

I ended up having a wonderful time smiling and laughing with these nice women.

The more you heal, the easier it is to welcome these triggers and say thank you.

At that time, I realized how much healing I had done.

That contributed to how quickly I rebounded from that trigger.

The more you heal, the easier it will be to show up as you.

The less fear you have, the less you will be worried about what others think.

When you are living in your authenticity, you will be able to feel good as you.

You won't try to be or show up the way others expect you to.

The more healing you do, the easier it will be to show your true authenticity.

Reflection Questions and Actions:

1. On a scale of 1-5, 5 being the highest, where does your self-confidence fall?
2. What steps have you been taking to heal your heart from past trauma?
3. What areas do you not want to touch, or ones that make you the most uncomfortable when it comes to healing? These are the areas that often need healing the most.

You will find the light by going into the dark. That is how you will truly get to know the true you.

I'm not saying you have to open the door fully, reliving past traumas. Instead, I'm saying acknowledge those feelings that you've buried deep within, and look at how that trauma helped change your life in a positive way. Often, a painful, traumatic experience brings you to where you are meant to be, putting you on the right path.

If you have been sexually or physically abused or assaulted, I encourage you to seek professional help with a trained Psychologist or Therapist. You should be under the proper care to connect to your past trauma.

Think about a time when you have shared your authentic self with others and how it felt to show up as you without a mask.

Trying to be and do what people expect of you can be exhausting.

Picture a time when you felt free to be you in your entirety, and how good it felt to not worry about what others think.

Pillar Four: Authenticity.

What does it mean to live in your authenticity?

It means that you are showing the world who you really are without a mask.

You show up as you, letting go of the need for validation from others to make you feel loved and accepted.

You no longer need anyone's approval, except for your own.

You stop worrying about being judged by others.

You stop comparing yourself to others because you understand that this is your journey, unique to you.

I still put up those personal posts on social media, sharing my life with everyone.

I don't need anyone's approval.

If I'm guided to share a message, then I know it needs to be shared.

Whether people comment, like, or love my post doesn't matter to me.

What matters is that the people who need to see this message see it.

I am going to dive much deeper in authenticity further in this book. For now, it's important to understand that the more you show up, get out of your comfort zone, learn to say no, focus on your well-being, and your healing work, the more your authenticity will come shining through.

The more comfortable you become in your own skin, the less other people's opinions will matter. You won't care about looking silly or like you don't know what you are doing.

Over time, you learn to live in your authenticity the majority of the time.

It's okay to have moments where you will still feel insecure or question yourself.

It doesn't matter how much you grow or how much healing you've done over time, that is part of the human experience.

Give yourself kindness, compassion, and grace.

Your job is to recognize when you have moments where you feel inauthentic, using this as an opportunity to find out what is coming up for you internally.

Reflection Questions and Actions:

1. Think of a time when you have been really comfortable in your own skin, and showed up as you?
   - How did that feel?
   - What do you think made this time different from others when you were not able to show up as you?
   - Take small steps every day to live in your authenticity.
   - Start getting real with yourself.

2. Ask yourself what areas are you stuck in? Where do you need help?

3. What areas can you show up more as you? For example, speaking up in a work meeting or with friends. Take the lead on a project or planning a get together.

When you do more of the inner healing work, it will become easier to forgive yourself and those who have hurt you in the past. When you start to understand that these life experiences are all happening for you, to grow you, help you heal, and prepare you for what you are called to in life, you will see that forgiveness is an important part in your journey.

Pillar Five: Forgiveness.

When you haven't truly forgiven yourself and or others who have hurt you, you can get stuck.

Forgiveness is very powerful and can move boulders that have kept you where you are.

When you hold on to all the hurt, anger, frustration, and sadness, you are keeping yourself from letting go and creating a new and improved reality. Part of you may still be stuck in the past, not able to let go of feeling wronged, or maybe you even blame yourself on some deep level for what happened.

Maybe you think that you should have known better. *"Why did I stay in this situation for so long?"* You may have buried your feelings so deep down that you don't even realize that they are still there, until now.

Give yourself grace, kindness, and compassion.

Forgiveness is important in your growth, but it can be tough to truly forgive.

Forgiveness is part of healing and the way to the love within your own heart.

Those who were in a long-term committed relationship with a narcissist may find it difficult to forgive due to all the pain they caused you.

All the years that you dealt with this abuse are gone, and there may be anger towards yourself for staying so long, believing that he could change, and wanting to see the best in him even when he showed his worst.

It is imperative that you forgive yourself, too.

You did the best that you could. You put in the effort all the time, having tried everything to make the marriage or relationship work.

It's not your fault. You are a good person who deserves much love, respect, honesty, kindness, compassion, and support.

By forgiving yourself and him, you will be creating space for a deeper level of healing as well as space for new love to enter.

Although you may want to stay closed off because the thought of letting anyone else into your heart may be unbearable, I encourage you to stay open, and ask God and or the Universe to prepare you for that right person.

God will do just that as He's been doing with me.

If you stay closed off to true love and a healthy relationship, you are letting the narcissist win. Do you really want to do that?

Why suffer more or keep yourself from someone amazing?

Take the time to heal, grow, open that beautiful heart of yours, and allow love to come into your world.

Be open to all of the possibilities around you, and stay open to love.

Reflection Questions and Actions:

1. Start small and ask yourself, "What do I need to forgive myself for?" Maybe something happened and you were being hard on yourself just the other day even. Give yourself kindness, compassion, and grace choosing to forgive yourself.

2. Who do I still need to forgive? Have I truly forgiven myself?

- Who else needs my forgiveness? It's about you! Forgiving helps you get unstuck, opens your heart more, and walks you towards that beautiful, blessed life.

3. Some of you have moved on, and found a much healthier relationship. Ask yourself, have I really let this man into my heart? Do I still have walls up? We will dive into this more later.

4. What can I do to let this person in more? Start to think about this.

How can I take more of my walls down to bring more of who I am to the surface?

What barriers do you put up to protect yourself?

Loving You

"Love is the great miracle cure. Loving ourselves works miracles in our lives."
—Louise Hay

Why Loving You is so Important.

Loving yourself is a game changer.

How often have you heard that you need to love yourself more?

There is a reason that you keep receiving this message. The Law of Attraction says that you attract what you are. You may argue, "*How can that be? I'm not a narcissist.*"

Try to keep an open mind here.

The narcissist doesn't really love himself, is insecure, and wants someone to love him.

He wants to be adored, praised, and to feel so good about himself. That's what he needs you for – to feed his ego.

He pushes that love away, and is incapable of giving and receiving love.

He is searching for that one person to fulfill his needs because he cannot fulfill his own needs.

I know that is a lot to digest.

How does this tie to you?

Be honest with yourself.

Either at the time of the relationship and/or now, how much do you love yourself?

How insecure were you or are you now?

Were you and/or are you looking for a man who will love you, making you feel truly loved and accepted? You may want to take some time to absorb that.

You attract that which is of the same vibrational frequency that you are. If you find and grow the love within you more, then you will attract a secure man who loves himself in a healthy way.

You won't get sucked in by the charm and lure of the narcissist because you won't need adoration early on. You are already receiving love from you.

Start working on the relationship with you to fill the void you feel. It's not going to be filled in any outside relationship.

Make the decision today to truly start loving yourself at a whole new level. It's time to discover the amazing in you.

Date yourself, spend time with you, and connect to your heart.

My Struggle with Self-Love in Childhood

Because of my childhood experiences, I struggled with self-love for a long time.

I grew up in a nice neighborhood with parents who are still married. They had this happy marriage where they were each other's best friend. They spent all of their free time together, sharing a love for tennis, their children, and other hobbies.

They didn't spend time with their own friend groups, so I didn't see any separate interests.

I had a great example of what a loving marriage looked like, so why did I struggle so much with relationships?

Like me, you see life through the filter of your experiences and beliefs.

Like so many, I unconsciously, unknowingly, created limiting beliefs as young as six years old.

My father was affectionate and said, "I love you often." I knew and felt that I was loved. He traveled for work, and was often flying across the US building a National Sales Team. He worked hard to provide a good life for his family.

My father was patient, loving, and kind as I was growing up. When I was in high school, he spent a couple of years consulting from home. I loved how he taught me how to drive and cook. This helped me to really bond with my father.

As I got older, I thought that a relationship would fulfill me, and make me feel loved. I wanted that male attention that I missed out on for years.

My mother was home with me and my younger brother while my father was traveling. They had a close relationship. My brother could do no wrong in my mother's eyes. He had this way of diffusing any situation and making her laugh.

I didn't feel that same connection with my mother. Looking back over the years, I clearly see that her love language, based on the book The Five Love Languages, was Acts of Service. She was always taking care of me, showing her love that way. As a child, I didn't understand that. She didn't say "I love you" and I felt unloved. It turns out that her mother showed her love the same way because it was all she knew.

I created a story of never feeling good enough, and being unworthy of love, which in turn became my belief well into my thirties.

My mother wanted the best for me and truly wanted me to be happy. She was only trying to help, but I saw it as not being smart or popular enough. Since she was a math teacher, she would help with my math homework, but I put a wall up, becoming frustrated because I was insecure. I felt judged, but it turned out I was judging myself.

My mother was actually never judging me.

It took a long time before I developed an amazing relationship with my mother. As I healed over the years, that is exactly what happened.

Growing up, when my father was home, I watched my mother cater to him. She would hand him the remote so he could choose what to watch on TV. She would ask him what he wanted for dinner or which restaurant to go to.

To this day, my mother is still amazed that being so easygoing is what I learned from her. In my relationships, I typically didn't have an opinion. Often, I heard that I didn't know who I was or that I wasn't comfortable in my own skin.

I hated to hear that.

I just didn't care which restaurant we went to.

I didn't learn to speak up or share my thoughts, opinions, and what I wanted till I turned forty.

I shared where I wanted to go more with friends, but that was different.

Doing this in romantic relationships was where I struggled.

Late Bloomer

Being in three high schools and two colleges in different states contributed to me being a late bloomer. I didn't have my first date until I was a freshman in college, and it was a fairytale–like date.

We met as I was flying home. He went to Cornell while I was at Ithaca College, both in Ithaca, NY. He was already planning all the things we would do in the future together. I felt special and that was a feeling that I desired.

Then it happened….

One night, he gave me a hug goodnight and then, to my surprise, we didn't go out again.

The next year, I followed my parents to California, transferring to a private college, University of the Pacific. There I met "Mike", my best guy friend who was like having a boyfriend in so many ways, except it was plutonic.

We would smile, laugh, and flirt all the time. Everyone was waiting for us to start dating, but we never did. We even spent time with each other's families. This was so confusing to me that I questioned my self-worth, and thought," *I'm not worthy of being loved."*

Also, I had become close friends with another guy, and the two of them would fight for my attention to win me over, but then it was only about winning.

The prize was to win me, but not actually date me.

I clearly didn't understand boys or guys at all.

Each experience with a guy led me to believe that something was wrong with me.

I Feel Unloved and Unwanted

After college, I wasn't any less confused. My boyfriend at the time didn't show up when I cooked a nice dinner. He decided he would apologize later and hang out with his friends.

One time, I was really sick, and needed him to pick up some medicine for me. He said he would do it after work. A friend of mine had to go to the store for me because I couldn't wait any longer. In the end, I chose me and that decided I deserved to be treated better. Years later, he sent me an apology email saying how sorry he was for the way he treated me. He truly felt awful about it.

I often chose emotionally unavailable guys who were not ready for a relationship. They may have started out great, but they all went in the same direction. It was always the guy who just got out of a long-term relationship or who was hurt terribly by someone he loved. Because of this, I created stories and beliefs that guys would disappoint me and I would be abandoned in some way.

I didn't feel worthy of being loved and didn't understand why I was so hard to love.

I wasn't meeting men who were like my father. I so badly wanted a fairytale romance where we loved each other and enjoyed each other's company, always on the same page.

Looking back, I realize that this was unrealistic. Each relationship is unique and I shouldn't have tried to recreate what my parents had.

I was also choosing men who I felt unloved and judged by, which was the story I created around my mother. My way of trying to earn my mother's love through hearing "I love you" in a relationship, which I rarely heard, was through these unhealthy relationships..

Wake Up Call

Having had such a healthy upbringing, I wondered how on earth I ended up with such a warped view on love. Where did the notion that I wasn't worthy of love come from?

I wanted to be loved so badly that I stayed in a long-term, unhealthy, narcissistic relationship with Greg. I wanted to earn his love and thought that, if I tried harder, he could really love me.

Looking back, I see how truly unhealthy that was.

I got tired of the tears, the pain, and the emotional abuse, so one day I left.

Two things got me to this point.

The first thing was my little dog Chloe. On Memorial Day 2011, I was with Greg and his parents at a state park, where we took the dogs for a walk. It had been such a beautiful day and I actually was feeling relaxed and good, which was rare for me.

All of a sudden, this man yelled, "Pick up your dogs, pick up your dogs." Greg picked up his dog and had his back to me. I was holding her when this Rottweiler came up to me. He pulled her down by the foot, right out of my arms.

I'm only 5'4, so there wasn't much I could do to defend myself. I felt alone, in shock, and completely helpless in the moment. There on the ground was my little six-pound dog, her white fur stained with blood as she slid her body across the asphalt trying to get to safety.

The owner came over to get his dog and, at the same time, Greg came over to pick Chloe up off the ground. Her foot was dangling and her yellow bow was still in her hair. Greg proceeded to yell at me, asking, *"Why didn't you pick her up?"* He was blaming me. The bystanders who had been watching said I was holding the little dog.

Greg vented at me, it appeared that he was feeling incredibly guilty for what just happened. We walked quickly to the car with his parents so that we could rush Chloe to the emergency vet. The vet cleaned her up and bandaged her, letting us know that we should take her to UC Davis Veterinary Hospital, one of the best in the country. That stop probably saved her life, having treated the infection from the dog bite immediately.

At UC Davis, the doctors called me back to the exam room, explaining the prognosis and telling me her treatment options. I was heartbroken and tears streamed down my face. I didn't want to remove her foot. She danced on her hind legs, so I couldn't do that.

I opted to save her foot with surgery, bone grafts, and pins would be placed for three months.

Chloe spent her first birthday in the hospital and the doctors and staff took such good care of her. My little munchkin, as I call her, was such a sweetheart. After the infection cleared, they were able to do the surgery. I had her since she was eight weeks old and was very attached. Her surgery went smoothly and eventually she came home.

Once home, she needed round-the-clock care. Everything had to revolve around Chloe's schedule.

Greg seemed incredibly jealous of Chloe taking center stage. I spent more time at home taking Chloe to her weekly vet visits. Fortunately, my father helped because I was very busy with work at the time. For a long time, I felt incredibly guilty for this wake-up call. Seeing that it took Chloe going through such a traumatic event to open my eyes to the harsh reality of the life I had signed up for hurt me badly.

I'm truly grateful that what happened woke me up. She truly saved me from marrying him. In the end, when she had finally healed, he said, "Now that she is healed, we should give her to your parents as a present, since they love her so much." I realized that this man would have me give away my own baby! I would never choose him over her.

The second thing was talking to a close friend of mine who really had my best interests at heart. At the time, I had moved in with Greg.

My condo sale had gone through despite taking several months. It was all already in motion, and he promised things would be different moving forward. We were looking at houses, and he told realtors and homeowners we met that we were engaged, even though he hadn't proposed yet.

My friend said, "One day, you are going to blow your pretty little brains out if you stay with this man." I couldn't stop crying after she painted this horrific picture. I knew she was right about me coming to hate myself and not seeing the point of living. Not to say I would actually have done that, but I wanted to disappear.

I had plenty of moments where I was driving and I was so unhappy that I thought, *"Would the world be better off without me?"*

I never really wanted to hurt myself. I just wanted to make the pain stop and disappear.

I didn't really think that I would be missed at the time.

The world would go on.

I kept going, though, and knew that I could create a better life for myself – one that I loved.

That life of discovering passions and interests and finding happiness does exist.

I shared these important key moments in my life to show you how unloved, unhappy, unfulfilled, and unworthy I felt.

It took time to heal, grow, do the inner work, find my self-worth, and to love myself.

I'm telling you that, if I can go from where I was and heal, love myself, find my voice, step into my personal power, and be brave enough to follow my calling, then so can you.

See? I'm no more special than any of you reading this book. I got tired of the way things were, I said, "Enough! I'm ready to grow, change, and to do the work to reclaim my heart power." Learning to love myself is what helped me to find the power within to heal and to step into my personal power.

Growing Your Self Love

Now let's talk about growing your self -love.

Growing your self- love is a true game changer in all aspects of your life.

Everywhere you turn, someone says, "You need to love yourself."

How do you know where you are in your journey to self- love? This is something I wondered for some time.

I knew over a decade ago that I had learned to love my inner child.

Over the years, I had to love myself to heal but it was more of an obligation. It felt like something I HAD to do. I was single for eight years and had come to the point of giving up. I only went out on a handful of dates during that time, but for the most part, I stayed away from men all together.

I was done, having decided that there was no one for me, and that I would be better off alone. I spent this time really getting to know me, growing, and loving myself more.

I loved myself enough to not chase my boyfriend, Jeff, after he broke up with me in December 2021, right before Christmas. I knew, as did he, that I was amazing, having all these qualities that he loved, and we had so much in common. We just weren't amazing together as it wasn't the right fit.

I saw this as an opportunity to get crystal clear on what I wanted in the right relationship, and I looked at what wasn't the right fit here. I was tired of intensity and God was showing me that I needed consistency instead, a no rush kind of love.

Over the years, my self- worth, self-confidence, and self-love grew. I had done a lot of inner healing work, got to the point of enjoying my own company, and knew all these wonderful qualities that I brought to the table.

During my Spiritual Awakening in January 2022, I fell in love with myself. It was a whole new place to be. I started to love my life, not needing to be a part of anyone else's. I was dating myself. I would go do the things that I wanted and, when I saw happy couples, I began to celebrate them.

Gabby Bernstein would call this driftwood, and say that you are attracting love into your life, and that love is all around you.

I stopped being impatient while wondering when it was going to be my turn. I didn't go back to an old pattern of, "It's never going to happen for me." Instead, I envisioned the love I so desired.

I connected to how I felt in those moments, how we felt, and I could see our love so clearly. I started to create this new reality in my imagination, knowing and believing that one day this or something better would come into my physical reality.

Self- Care

Over the years, I learned the importance of self -care.

I had a number of painful lessons in this area, but eventually I mastered the repeated lessons.

Intentional self- care shows that you love yourself. Meditating, moving your body, going for a walk, being in nature, taking a relaxing bath, drinking your cup of coffee in peace just for you, and journaling are some examples of self-care.

Self-care is anything that makes you feel good that you are doing primarily for you.

Focus on making yourself a priority. You are far more effective at helping others when you are at your best, so fill your cup. No one wants to drink from a half empty cup.

Be an example for those around you to say, "I'm worth it. What is important to me matters, too."

Speak Kindly to Yourself

Speaking kindly to yourself and accepting compliments shows that you love yourself.

It's about getting out of your own way, allowing good to enter your life, letting go of the need to self- sabotage, shows that you love yourself.

Look in the mirror and ask what you like about yourself or love about yourself. Start with physical features and then move to internal qualities.

Start showing yourself the kind of love and affection you deserve.

It all starts with you.

When you are kind to yourself, you will attract people, especially men, into your life who will be kind and loving as well.

Celebrate Your Wins

Celebrating your big and small wins will grow your self- love.

You were meant to be your biggest champion. While being with a narcissist, you have been told not to be boastful, brag, or that you are full of yourself when you got excited about your accomplishments or wins.

I'm saying celebrate every single one of them! God wants you to see and finally believe just how amazing you truly are.

What do your small wins look like?

You could have been patient instead of getting frustrated driving in traffic to work that day.

You made time to watch your favorite movie.

You made it to the gym and worked out.

You scheduled time for a walk, and to sit in nature.

You journaled and or meditated for ten minutes.

You stayed calm in a situation that in the past would have upset you.

Your favorite ice cream flavor was available today at the shop.

You tried a new activity, went to a different coffee shop, or grocery store.

You got out of your comfort zone with one small step.

Set Healthy, Loving Boundaries

Setting loving, healthy boundaries shows that you love yourself.

Setting boundaries helps you to protect you and your energy. Saying yes to everyone and everything will one day lead to burn out.

Ask yourself, "Is *this something that I really need to do? Is someone else able to complete this task or assignment?"*

When you do everything for everyone, they don't learn their lessons.

They don't grow and expand their knowledge. Learn to say no, and put yourself first.

Boundaries look like, *"I will turn off my electronics one hour before I go to bed, so that I can relax."* You could set a particular time as well.

Another example is, *"I am free to talk Tuesday between 6-7 pm or Thursday between 7-8 pm."*

It is so important to protect your energy and your well- being.

The Power of Your Own Love

The more you love yourself, the bigger your heart will open.

When you come home to the love within your heart, the power within you will be awakened.

You were born out of love, and love is your birthright.

Love is all around you! It's in your heart, your soul, and it's what will bring you to your purpose or calling when the time is right.

Love will literally heal your heart, allowing you to feel whole.

Keep finding ways to show yourself more love each day. Before you know it, that beautiful heart of yours will bloom like a rose opening each petal.

A feeling of peace and freedom will wash over you as you finally discover the key to unlock your own heart.

Reflection Questions and Actions:

1. Think back, what was it that caused you to leave your unhealthy, narcissistic, emotionally abusive relationship?
2. At the time on a scale of 1-5, 5 being the most loved. How much did you love yourself? How did you feel about you at the time?
3. What steps did you take to grow your self-love, feeling more worthy, overall, better about yourself?
4. Do you feel stuck to move forward in life? How so, and in which areas?
5. As of today, on a scale of 1-5, 5 being the highest. How much do you love yourself today? How much better do you feel about where you are today? There are no right or wrong answers. Be honest with yourself as that is what will ultimately move you forward to where you want to go.
6. What are you currently doing to grow your self- love in each of these areas? Which areas do you want to improve, or spend more time on?

    ___ Self-Care

    ___ Speaking Kindly to Yourself

    ___ Complimenting Yourself

    ___ Celebrating your Small and Big Wins

    ___ Setting Healthy, Loving Boundaries

7. Plan a day once a week where you can write down your small and big wins. Give yourself a small reward once you complete this task. Positive reinforcement will help this to become a habit more quickly. This will also make it more fun.

My relationship coach had my group once a week actually post 3 insights, 3 wins, and 3 things we were each working on for next week. I found this to be a great way to stay on track while celebrating my accomplishments. If you feel called, this is a great activity for you as well.

It is crucial for you to learn to be your biggest fan.

Faith and Trust

"The More Energy and Intention I Bring to my Faith the more Fearless I AM."
—Gabby Bernstein

You Are Never Alone

No matter what your faith, it is important to understand that you aren't alone. There is support and guidance all around you every day. It is just a matter of learning to tap in and be aware of all the signs and guidance around you. You can say God, Spirit, the Universe, Angels, Higher Self, Higher Power, or whatever you believe in. All that matters is that you understand that you are loved, guided, protected, and supported always.

My Religious Upbringing

I grew up Roman Catholic. My mom would basically drag my brother and I to church on Sunday mornings.

We didn't attend a children's Sunday school like a lot of other kids. Instead, we would sit through what I would call an adult mass.

I never wanted to be there, and didn't feel connected to church as a child. Being Catholic, everything went through the priest. I learned that I could pray, but I never expected to hear or see any response.

I grew up thinking this was a one way only communication with God. I would pray and hope my prayer would be answered. Being Catholic, I would have to take a religious after school class once a week. We went through the stories from the Bible and I learned what I was supposed to.

At fourteen, I had the opportunity to play tennis at a club. The club had a ladder system where I would play weekly matches with other kids. I was excited for two reasons – I loved tennis and I didn't have to go to church on Sundays anymore. I didn't like to be forced to do things and was very stubborn as a kid. This gave me a choice, which made me feel good, feeling that what I wanted mattered.

That was the end of my religion for years.

My parents raised both my brother and I to be good people. I treated others kindly, seeing everyone as an equal. I didn't cheat, lie, or steal. I've never even smoked a cigarette or tried any kind of drug. I was straight laced, as it was referred to back then.

Over the years, it got to the point where I rarely prayed.

From a young age, I was mercilessly picked on by the girls at school and it lasted till after junior high. It was the worst in elementary school, having left scars I had to heal much later in life.

God had given me good parents, a brother who at the time I didn't get along with, a good job, my independence, and a condo.

Later, He gave me a house I bought, and close friends, so what more could I ask for?

None of it really made me happy though, and I only felt fulfilled at certain times, as it would ebb and flow.

"*Isn't that just life?*" I would ask myself. I appreciated all that I had even before I learned to be grateful.

On the flip side, I definitely focused on what was missing and had a lack mentality. Either that, or I was content and living life in the status quo.

Life Was Happening to Me

For many years, I saw life as happening to me.

The idea of it happening for me never registered till my early 40s.

I thought that I had to settle.

I was successful in my career, making good money on a job that so many people would want, so I can't have it all.

"I'm meant to be good at my job, to spend all my time working because that's where I'm getting validation from."

I made my choices, and was on my path.

I was in medical sales, calling on hospitals.

I did this for almost my entire career until I left at 44 years old.

People wanted my job and my life because I had so much.

They would only see it from the outside, not what really happened behind closed doors at work.

They didn't see all that I gave up to be successful at that career – the stress, the burn out, the experiences I missed out on being such a workaholic, the emotional toll of how badly I was treated at times at work, the people pleasing, saying yes at my own expense, and putting myself and my well-being last.

I had taken this road, doing the math on how many more years it would be before I could retire to collect my pension and 401K.

I wondered how many years I could stay in this career, living this way, feeling unfulfilled. I didn't know how to change it.

There were amazing moments, too.

I loved winning, being on stage, being one of the best in the country, going on fancy awards trips, and being chosen to sit next to the CEO at a banquet and the founder's grandson.

I had arrived!

On that last awards trip, I went from sitting next to the CEO and the Executive Vice President offering to mentor me to going through a painful acquisition.

I Had to Make You Uncomfortable So You Would Move

Shortly after this trip, I found myself dealing with a new manager coming in as mine retired. At first, I had high hopes for this new manager. Before I knew it, their leadership took over our business unit, even though we had acquired their company.

I no longer fit in with the way this group did business as I was asked to do things that I considered unethical. The higher executives who were previously there to support me either retired or had left.

That was the writing on the wall, telling me that I should get out. I had been here for over ten years and I didn't know anything else.

This manager proceeded to make up fake customer complaints about me and sent me a letter to discuss my performance. I was completely heartbroken, livid, hurt, and my blood was boiling all in one. I contacted HR and sent a letter letting them know what had happened.

I quickly learned that the company was going to take care of their managers. All that I sacrificed over the years didn't matter at all.

The realization that I had given up so much hit me like a ton of bricks.

I consulted an employment law attorney who I ended up hiring to protect my rights.

I then took a leave of absence because I was so sick and run down from what I believed to be narcissistic behavior.

Sadly, this was familiar.

At my previous company, I had been moved to a new manager during a reorganization who I believed exhibited narcissistic tendencies.

He made up fake customer complaints and I was a top performer.

One of his complaints I pointed out was for a customer that wasn't even in my territory.

He basically copied and pasted someone else's performance review for another state. It still didn't matter.

On the bright side, I was able to get a small severance to leave with an acquisition coming up.

How did I end up being in this situation again all these years later?

After all that I had been through, my doctor put me on Zoloft for my anxiety. I had to send reports in during my leave of absence, visiting my doctor regularly.

This painful experience ended up being a gift.

Right away, I began to see that now I was able to finally find what I enjoyed and was passionate about in life.

At first, I had no idea how to fill my days without work, but then I started to live and appreciate being in the now. I didn't refer to it as that then. In fact, as I type this, I'm having that realization of living in the now moment is where that all first started for me.

My mind calmed down, and I started to feel what I would now refer to as peace enter. At the time, I felt less stress and began to enjoy myself more.

I learned the importance of slowing down.

A Gift from God

Looking back, I know this was a gift from God meant to open my eyes and put me on the right path.

God had to make me uncomfortable so that I would move.

I'm grateful to that manager for behaving that way because it moved me forward, and got me unstuck from a life that no longer fit – one that I was outgrowing.

All of the lessons have turned out to be blessings, opening new doors, moving me forward, stretching me to grow, and ultimately preparing me for my destiny, calling, or purpose in life.

At the time, I was very angry, and I had to work through that. In time, I found peace and was able to forgive him. After my leave ended, I had to go back to work, which was incredibly painful and scary.

The company who I slaved away for over a decade wouldn't even negotiate me out. They said that I could leave of my own free will if I chose. My attorney was needed to make sure that no one railroaded me out or played games.

I was a fighter and I chose to rise, as opposed to just having left to make it easy on them. I waited to leave until I had a new job.

I looked for another medical sales job because that was all I knew.

What Patterns Do You See in Your Life?

At this point, let me ask you this, do you see a pattern here in what kept happening in my career?

Can you guess what is coming next?

At this time in my life, I didn't understand why the same thing kept happening to me repeatedly.

Yes, I'll say it happened to me because, at that moment, I didn't yet know how my beliefs, stories, and conditioning created the reality I was living in.

In other words, my life circumstances and this same story were getting ready to play out yet again.

How Did I Get Here Again?

I was a good person, so why did I keep ending up here?

I had a new manager or actor, let's label him narcissist – what number are we on now? I'm trying to laugh at this looking back.

My pattern was obvious only I didn't know it. I hadn't connected the dots of me being the common denominator here.

I believed this next one to be narcissist manager number three in my career.

It all started out promising, like the beginning of a movie or romance with a narcissist. Even as a manager, he seemed fine, and at least I was free.

I had to get out.

Looking back at the first interview, they played good cop, bad cop, and can you guess which my manager was? Yes, you've got it. The bad cop.

I should have known what was coming. Interviews with leadership who he reported to were cold, impersonal, and made me feel like I was a bother. They both wanted to get these interviews done quickly to get the position filled. Definitely not a welcoming environment.

Here I was, free from my last nightmare situation, and hopeful of what's to come.

Once I finished the arduous training of multiple trips across the country, being away for weeks, COVID started.

I didn't have access to hospitals.

California was locked down for months.

My manager had my entire sales team on a call with his area director going through my sales opportunities.

I was asked (what I would consider) to lie or make up sales opportunities.

. I had to move unrealistic opportunities up in the sales cycle, spinning a story.

I said that I wasn't comfortable doing that.

I wasn't going to compromise my values. I'm not saying that, in the past, I didn't stretch the truth or tell a little white lie in these cases, but I was no longer able to do that.

In this case, I didn't even have the relationships and hadn't even been able to meet with most of these people in the hospitals. I was dealing with competitive accounts, so I was going to be 100 percent forthright.

I stayed firm on being honest while I got berated, belittled, and treated horribly on this call that everyone was listening to. My manager then called me asking what he was going to do with me. He asked if I thought this was acceptable looking at my lack of opportunities. He proceeded to give me one more chance before he put me on a performance plan.

This experience was tough for me as I was used to being a top performer. Now I felt humbled, insecure, and had no idea what I was doing. I completely lost my self-confidence.

At this time, I completely surrendered, something I never did before. I didn't even know this word back then, but looking back here, I was choosing to wave a white flag.

I surrendered right there and said, "*I know I don't deserve to be treated this way. I'm not signing up for this again, and wherever the chips fall I'll be okay.*" It was during COVID and I truly didn't care. I went away for a long weekend with a close friend and her family to their cabin at the last minute. It was just what I needed.

What just happened? How did I end up in the same place again?

I was no longer that person who was a people pleasing workaholic who didn't have a life outside of work.

I no longer wanted to push and make everything happen in the business world.

I had softened during my leave of absence, and after the painful lessons, I learned that my sanity, self-care, and self-worth were far more important than this job.

I no longer embodied this high -powered salesperson. I was always honest with my customers, and could ask for the business. I had a strong follow through, holding anyone's hand through it all for as long as it was needed to bring the customer on board and get them through the transition period. I worked on these long six-month to one- year projects when I sold products and solutions to a hospital. It was all about relationship selling for me.

I was never going to be this cutthroat rep, and I never had to be that way in order to be a top performer in my life.

I wasn't going to change now.

In Full Surrender

As I fully surrendered, honestly not caring about the outcome, my manager came back. This time, he asked me if I wanted to switch teams and move to current and new customers instead. I agreed.

Looking back, I fully believe God was responsible. He didn't want me to leave because He had a gift for me.

My next manager, "Ben", helped put me back together.

My confidence was shot, and I felt completely broken.

He was kind and patient with me at that time.

He helped me to celebrate my small wins and, at the time, I thought very highly of him.

I never would have expected him to exhibit narcissistic behavior, and I believed that he was pushing me out of the company.

I did everything to take care of the company and my customers.

Fast forward two and a half years later.

Could my pattern seriously be any clearer?

Do you see a similar pattern in any aspect of your life?

Why I'm walking you through my painful lessons and patterns in my career

After seeing my experiences, I want to help you understand where your patterns are. Then you can tell what is not working in your life. When you continue to have the same experiences, it's like being in a loop or stuck on the same level of a video game.

You have the power to move to that next level at any time you decide you are ready by breaking the pattern and ending the loop.

How can you break the pattern? By choosing a new action, a different choice will result in a new outcome.

This new action will get you unstuck and help you move forward in a new direction into the unknown. This is where you get to write a new story.

Pick up that pen and start writing. You are the author of your life.

Your life is a choose your own adventure book. There are different paths to take and no one path is better than the others.

You will have God, Spirit, Angels, and/or the Universe supporting and guiding you along the way.

Signs and Guidance

It wasn't until my Spiritual Awakening in January of 2022 that my life completely changed in regards to my faith.

It was in early January when my relationship coach told me to pray or ask God and the Universe for what I wanted.

I said, "I want peace, love, and joy." He told me to scream it out loud. That's what I did.

That day, I was crying in the shower when I begged screaming for peace, love, and joy. I realized there had to be more meaning in life, and I wanted to feel more fulfilled.

A friend who I hadn't seen in a few years contacted me and asked me to go to church with her. I said, "Okay. Why not?" I felt connected to peace, love, and joy (the fruits of the spirit) as they showed up on the slides in the service. Then the pastor showed the ego was filled with anxiety and chaos.

I was tired of living that way and all I knew is that I was ready for peace. I had enough of trying to figure out my life, and now it was time to surrender, taking my hands off the wheel like the Carrie Underwood song, "Jesus Take the Wheel."

All of a sudden, I began to connect with everything around me and find deep meaning. I cried listening to this song as I was driving. Once again, but now in my car, I begged with tears down my face for peace, love, and joy.

A moment later, a Pandora Station that I had never downloaded before started to play on the radio.

It was Peaceful Morning Radio, and the first song was "Joy in the Morning".

The second song was "Do Not Fear, You Are Blessed", a Christian Song. Right then, it was a clear sign to go back to this Christian Church.

I began to see signs everywhere all around me.

I started to see angel wings above my house and in my neighborhood, crosses wherever I turned, kind people surrounded me, and I saw God in all of it.

For someone who had just found her faith, this was a new experience for me.

I very quickly saw just how loved, protected, guided, and supported I was at every moment.

I never knew that kind of support was available to me. I had never welcomed it in.

I didn't know until then that I could have a personal relationship with God. I certainly didn't know that I would get all of these clear answers and responses back from him.

My life became truly magical.

I saw and felt love all around me.

I saw the world with fresh eyes….

The flowers were so vibrant, the sky various shades of blue, and the green grass looked even more brilliant.

I saw messages on license plates, on social media, delivered through people, songs, movies, TV, and I knew which ones were meant for me.

I began to trust the guidance all around me.

It became clear what time I needed to leave my house, where to go, what to do and, for the first time, I knew that I was always where I was supposed to be at the right moment. This was such a beautiful new way to live, feeling my way into everything, learning to get out of my head. Experiencing the present moment and taking it all in, appreciating everything around me – I had found peace.

After some geography changes at work, I was moved to a new manager. In early Spring 2021, I ended up with a Spiritually Awakened manager who was a true gift. He embodied peace, was centered, calm, and like no manager I had ever had.

For ten years of my career, I had a manager who was a kind, good person.

But, he was not centered, calm, or peaceful. I learned from "Brent" how to find inner peace and not let outside situations affect my peace. I saw how calmly he handled everything. There could be a huge crisis in a hospital and he took a deep breath, said that we will figure it out, and he wasn't rattled at all.

I'm grateful he was there to guide me through my Spiritual Awakening.

Further along, he helped me through some bumps and challenges on my path. I also loved that I could share all the exciting moments, too, as he was so supportive of it all. He had this calm confidence about him, and he had a big impact on my life. He is still supportive of my journey till this day.

You Are Worthy of a Beautiful, Blessed Life

Every one of you is worthy of a beautiful, blessed life.

Once you believe that it is possible for you to create all that was placed on your heart, you will move forward on your path.

It takes trust and faith that you are being guided and supported each step of the way. The signs are everywhere.

For example, say you keep seeing or hearing pickleball.

That's probably a sign for you to go learn pickleball. Signs are right in front of you, but they are easy to miss if you are always in your head, as opposed to being in the moment.

Next time you are out, look around you, be very present, and you will probably see messages that are meant for you. Once you start to see these signs, you will notice that guidance is always available to you.

Reflection Questions and Actions:

1. After reading this chapter look at the patterns in your life. Do you see a similar pattern where you keep reliving an almost identical situation like my narcissistic managers, where I was being pushed out? It can be in any aspect of your life. Be a detective and find the clues to solve the case in your life.

2. Is there something in your life that clearly isn't working? What is it? How can you go about making a change to break that pattern or loop?
3. Who has been a huge support system in your life? Who are you grateful for? Who encourages you to keep going, learning, and growing? This is the person you want in your corner as you walk forward, getting out of your comfort zone to the beautiful and blessed life that you desire.
4. Where do you feel unfulfilled in your life?
   If you could do anything, what would that be, and why?
   How would that make you feel?
5. On a scale of 1-5, 5 being the highest or most often, how often are you in your head, thinking, or overthinking?
6. How can you start to shift more to being present in the present moment?
7. Start to be more present in the now. Pay attention to the signs around you. Where are you being guided?

It's about seeing the sign three times or more, so consistently. If you see something once it's not a clear sign.

So often your signs and guidance are in plain sight. You never have to search for signs. They are right in front of you.

For example, you will be guided to go on social media and a post which resonates is at the top. Later, when you go back on it shows up again or a similar one.

Maybe you keep seeing Italy posts over and over. It may be a sign to take a trip to Italy. Maybe not now, but to be aware that an Italy trip is somewhere on the horizon.

Once you begin to identify your patterns and what isn't working, you can then shift your mindset to focus your energy on what you do want. Both your thoughts and your mindset will help you make the shift towards a beautiful, blessed life. You create your reality based on your thoughts, so why not move towards creating all that your heart desires? All you have to do is believe that the magic already exists within you in order to create that life.

Mindset to Magic

"Like the air you breathe, abundance in all things is available to you.
Your life will simply be as good as you allow it to be."
—Abraham Hicks

Shifting Your Mindset

Life will change in the most beautiful, yet powerful ways when you begin to see that a blessing can be found in each experience.

You may be asking yourself how is it a blessing when your heart was broken, you were treated badly in a relationship, or you lost so much time spending it with that person? The truth is that nothing is wasted. Each experience is here to teach you something, to learn, to grow, and to graduate from that lesson.

On to bigger and better things that are more aligned….

I have learned how important it is to show gratitude and appreciation for all of it, the good and the not so good experiences. Think back to some of the most challenging times of your life. What good came out of them?

In most cases, the experience taught you how strong and capable you are.

This allows you to grow and prepare you for what's coming in the future.

Learning to shift your mindset to see the lesson or blessing in each experience, changes the way you look at life.

There are no wrong turns in life.

You are here to learn, grow, make mistakes, try again, and experience all that life has to offer.

Know that you will get to where you are meant to be at the right time for you.

Lisa, my relationship coach, wanted me to keep going because I had made such great strides in my growth, having learned to love my inner child.

I wasn't ready for more.

Trust where you are at, and that you won't miss anything that's meant for you, even if it has to come in a round- about way.

This is so powerful, and will take the pressure off. Honor where you are in your life, or soul journey.

Another example of this is when I worked with my last relationship coach for a year.

I'd had my Spiritual Awakening and was taking leaps in my growth.

His wife wanted me to join her group to create my own business.

In other words, create my legacy and find my purpose.

I couldn't even imagine them then.

The whole thing overwhelmed me, and I just couldn't join.

Fast forward one and half years later...

I was guided to the right women to help me build my business, create my legacy, Reclaim Your Heart Power, to help women heal their hearts after narcissistic abuse and toxic relationships.

Helping women to open and heal their heart, find their voice, step into their personal power, so that they can walk into their soul mission or purpose....

I want women to feel fulfilled and realize that they are capable of anything that has been placed on their hearts, and that no dream is too big. It's all about timing.

Trust that the right people and resources will come along when the time is right. Sometimes the time is right, and you may not feel ready. That's okay.

If you hear a whisper or get signs to do something, or take that leap, then go for it.

It's all about learning to trust the inner guidance, the whisper of your soul.

Unwrapping a Gift

The emotionally abusive relationship I was in with Greg allowed me to finally realize that I had self-esteem issues, and that I didn't love myself. This one painful experience gave me the opportunity to wake up and make some big changes in my life. Little did I know at the time that this would end up being such an important part of my calling or soul mission. This was a necessary experience to find my own love, and sense of worthiness.

All of your experiences are here to help prepare you for your destiny and purpose.

Looking back, it makes so much sense as I can see the puzzle pieces all fitting together to shape me into who I've become today.

It's all in how you look at a situation. The man God guided me to in Spring 2023 was a huge gift.

Did I like experiencing emotional, what I believed to be narcissistic abuse for three days, going down the rabbit hole, questioning my beliefs, and feeling like I was losing my mind? Well, the answer is a big no. This short, yet painful lesson was one hundred percent worth it. I'm grateful that it was such a quick lesson because I had grown so much and had learned from my past. I knew I did not choose this, and that I deserved better, because I have been doing so much inner work, and could confidently say, "*I choose me.*"

I have unwavering faith, walking forward, knowing in my heart that God will bring me an amazing, loving, man who respects, and supports me. He's on the way, all in God's perfect, right, divine timing.

I'm truly grateful that this man God brought taught me so much. He gave me an opportunity to heal old wounds, break old patterns, and rise where God wanted me to be. He truly was a gift who has changed my entire life. This experience led me right into my soul mission – to help women heal their hearts after narcissistic abuse and toxic relationships.

When you look at my experience from this perspective, there are so many gifts here.

Reflection Questions and Actions:

1. Let's take a few minutes to go back to a time when you had a painful relationship or a painful time in your life. How can you reframe it to see the good in this experience? What did you learn in this lesson? You are free now! How does that feel? Are you able to see the gift in that alone? What good and blessings have come into your life now that you are no longer in that unhealthy situation? How does it feel to shift your mindset, seeing this painful time as a blessing or gift instead?

2. Practice reframing the thoughts that enter your mind.

   For example, *"I'm eating through my savings, since so many expenses have been coming up."*

   Reframe or change it to, *"I'm investing in myself, my family, my home, to make the improvements needed. It is worth it or I'm worth it."*

   Your well-being is always worth it, as I have learned. When you invest in yourself, it can last a lifetime.

3. Ask yourself in what area or areas should I invest more in? You are absolutely 100 percent worth the investment. For example, if you want to get fit and what you are doing on your own hasn't been working, then work with a trainer.

If you want to eat healthier, but need support, work with a nutritionist. If you want to heal, releasing pain and trauma, work with a coach or therapist. If you want to get unstuck, let go of old conditioning, past beliefs, and outdated stories, work with a coach, and or sign up for a program that fits your needs.

Investing in Myself

It took me a long time to realize that I needed to invest in myself.

Yes, I worked with relationship coaches.

I do remember my coach Lisa raising her prices substantially and I wasn't ready for the big jump. Plenty of other women were, and that also showed that they were ready to do more in depth work with her. If I recall correctly, her rate tripled and it was the perfect excuse for me to say no. I didn't see myself as worth the investment yet.

Eventually I still got there, many years later when I was ready to invest with a relationship coach 1:1 and their group program as well. I had to commit to three months, which then turned into a year when I renewed. It was a big jump for me at the time, but I knew and believed that I was worth the investment.

The Power of Now

Do you feel like your mind is often racing, where you have thoughts circling round and round, almost like a merry go round ride that you can't get off of? Typically, you have been programmed from a young age to overthink, try to figure things out, and rationalize.

Overthinking can be exhausting, and was certainly a habit for me for a very long time. It took time to make these shifts in my life. For so long, I would think about the past, wanting to rewrite parts that I didn't like how they played out. If I wasn't thinking about the past, then I was focused on the future. I would be so excited about an event, seeing a guy I was dating, plans with a friend, or a vacation, that I discovered that I was missing out on living in the moment. I just wanted to hit fast forward all the time. Does this sound familiar?

When you are focused on the past, you feel regret. Maybe you loved your life at one point and you often think back to when things were really great. Either way, both keep you trapped from moving forward and creating a beautiful, blessed life that you truly deserve.

On the flip side, when you focus on the future, then you may become anxious of the unknown or feel fearful. We have this innate need to want to know what is next.

"I'll be happy when I meet the right man."

"I'll be happy when I get that promotion or after I take the vacation I've been planning".

In reality, it's about being happy in the now moment. It is in the present where you will find joy and peace.

There are amazing things that happen each day when you slow down and pay attention.

There are wonderful people to meet, conversations to have, beautiful experiences to cherish, and messages and signs to receive.

When you are in such a hurry in your day, you miss most of these precious moments.

Slow down and take it all in.

Go take a walk for lunch in the park, put your feet in the grass feeling the earth, and or look around you.

What do you see?

What do you feel?

There is so much beauty in the world when you take a deep breath, stop, and appreciate it.

I get it. I was like you, constantly on the go, no time to slow down, having to get through my list.

You are missing out on truly living life when you stay in that mentality.

Your heart and your soul want you to go within, sit in the stillness, not checking your phone, and just breathe in the beautiful flowers, the green grass, the butterflies around you, and look up at the blue sky.

For so long, I didn't even see butterflies in real life because I was always hustling in get things done mode. Once I slowed down, I saw them everywhere. It is always such a beautiful sign in my day, one in which I'm truly grateful for.

That anxiety you feel could be from all the chaos in your life. Once you slow down, take some pressure off, realize that the world won't end if you don't get through your list today, you may feel calmer. It's worth a shot, right?

Just remember that you will not be able to undo decades of conditioning right away. It will take whatever time is right for you.

Keep taking small steps each day. It's about catching yourself, being aware of your thoughts, to be able to replace them with a new thought.

Choose Again

Early in 2022, when I joined Gabby Bernstein's Miracle Membership Group, I was reminded of one of her methods, the Choose Again Method, which I'll share here. I read about this method in her book *Super Attractor* in late 2019, but I hadn't applied it to my life until early 2022.

Choose Again Method:

- **Step 1: Notice the Thought.** Identify the negative thought. Being aware of your negative thoughts is how you are going to change them. Be kind to yourself, since being aware of a negative versus a positive thought is a huge first step.

- **Step 2: Forgive the Thought.** Basically, here you are forgiving yourself for having that negative thought. It's important to forgive yourself and not judge yourself for having that thought.

- **Step 3: Choose a New Thought, You Choose Again.** This gives you an opportunity to reach for a better feeling thought. For example, you have to be realistic. You can't go from being single to getting married overnight. Your thought is, *"I'm going to be alone. There aren't any good men out there for me"*. Say thank you and forgive yourself for that thought. Next, choose again. What is the next best feeling thought that you can reach for in this moment?" *I'm going to be open to dating quality men."* That might be as far in a positive direction that you can move in this moment. Next time, you can take another step, maybe focusing on what you can do to create a new outcome. *"I'm going to work with a relationship coach to better understand what I can do to meet quality men. I'm going to focus on more self-care and self-love to attract better men in my life."* See? Each step gets you further along in a more positive direction.

I decided it was time to continue to do things differently, keep getting out of my comfort zone, and take new actions. That's exactly what I did.

I had just been through an emotional breakup with my boyfriend the week before Christmas. At the time, I saw the gift and blessing in it, but I didn't know how to get him off my mind.

I committed myself to using the Choose Again Method every time I thought of him. I said, "Thank you, God and the Universe, for showing me what I don't want." Again, I chose a more positive thought, and I would insert a more positive thought. It's asking yourself what is the next best feeling thought that you can reach for right now.

For example, *"Thank you God and the Universe for showing me what I don't want – a boyfriend who is intense and lives in chaos. Instead, I choose a man who is consistent and peaceful. I choose again and I know that I'm worthy of a man who is ready and right for me."*

It took me two weeks of catching myself sixty times a day on average to stop thinking about my ex-boyfriend, and to learn how to focus on positive thoughts. Each time, I would shift my perspective to any thought that was more positive.

Catching myself every time I had a negative thought, I proceeded to shift to a more positive thought, ultimately rewiring my mind.

I've also chosen to learn to reframe my thoughts, which is something I've learned over the years at work.

Another example, but with using a reframing technique is you are dreading a work meeting later that day.

Instead reframe it to find something good in that experience.

It can be small. *"I'm looking forward to having cake at the work meeting today"*, or *"Oh good! I get to take a break to clear my head from the work project that I've been putting together."*

The best advice I can give is to put in as much effort in your growth and inner healing work as you do in your career and other areas of your life. The biggest investment you can ever make is in you. Aren't you worth it?

Many of you have put so much time, energy, and effort into your career or to staying at home taking care of your children. Just think if you could retrain your mind to see the good in your experiences, to shift your thoughts to a better one, to learn how to stop going down the rabbit hole when you begin spiraling. How would that change your life?

How to Create an Abundance Mindset

Focusing on what is already good in your life will bring in more abundance.

You've been conditioned to pay attention to what is missing, which is a lack mindset.

You may have a great job and wonderful friends, yet you focus on not being able to get into a healthy relationship with a man who truly loves you. It's so easy to fixate on what's missing in your life.

Of course, you want to fill in that empty space in hopes that you will feel complete with a sense of fulfillment.

How often do you get the promotion you want that you have worked so hard for, and then you just don't feel as fulfilled, excited, or as happy as you thought you would? This is why it's so important to connect within, so that you can see that you are already complete, and are a work of art.

Your happiness and fulfillment all stem from going within your heart and soul to connect with your true essence. Here you will find what your heart desires. The answers are all inside of you and not in the external world.

When you appreciate and focus your energy on what is already good and thriving in your life, you will create more of that abundance.

Start thinking about all the good in your life now.

Be grateful every day for what is thriving, and you will continue to see so much of what is thriving continue to show up in your day.

Why does this happen?

Why This Happens

Everything is made up of energy, including you, which is physics.

When you focus on the good in your life and are truly grateful, you vibrate at a higher energetic frequency.

Love, Appreciation, or Gratitude vibrate at the same high frequency.

Think about when you are happy and feel love in a relationship or something amazing happens in your life. People are attracted to that happy, grateful energy.

When you are having fun, people are often drawn to you. They feel your positive energy and want to be a part of it.

Same thing works for negative energy. It can be contagious.

How often have you had a friend or coworker who is having a bad day and upset? The more this person shares this negative energy with others, the more you may feel depleted and it could lower your vibrational frequency too, as well as the frequency of others around you.

Driftwood

Next time you get upset seeing happy couples everywhere you look, choose again.

Next time you get jealous because someone has the car, job, or promotion that you want, choose again.

Why is this such a game changer?

When you see what you truly desire that is in your heart, it is God and the Universe showing you that you are being aligned to what you desire. Gabby Bernstein refers to this as driftwood.

It is powerful to shift your mindset here and realize that you are receiving driftwood showing you that what you want is on its way. Now it's all about being patient. Just because you are seeing these signs doesn't mean that what you desire will appear right away.

Always focus on "It's on the way", instead of, "Why don't I have that?"

This is powerful when shifting your mindset. It could still be years away, but know that it's coming. That has been my experience.

I had to learn to be patient and surrender to the timing of it all, even though I saw endless signs every day for what was on its way to me. I can tell you that I know all of it has been worth the wait. It's important to always ask for this or something better when you pray or manifest what has been placed on your heart.

Reflection Questions and Actions:

1. When your mind is racing with thoughts about the past or future, hit pause. Then shift back to the present. Practice catching yourself and see how many times in one day you are focused on the past or future.

2. Are you more focused on the past or the future? What is coming up for you? Is it fearful or something that you are fondly remembering? If it's fearful, how can you see it with love? For example, what good came out of that tough experience? See something loving that came out of it.

3. Be in the now moment. Go outside and take a walk, choosing to be fully present in the moment. What do you see? What do you feel? How does your body feel when you focus on what is around you? This may feel strange as you probably aren't used to slowing down. Be kind and patient with yourself, since this is new for you to be fully present and aware of what is around you. Practice this daily.

4. Take a few deep breaths and come into the stillness within you. Let go of your thoughts and watch them pass by like clouds floating right by you. Close your eyes if you are somewhere where you feel safe. Then breathe in for a count of 4 seconds, hold for a count of 4 seconds, and breathe out for a count of 8 seconds. You can also try breathing in for 5 seconds, hold for 5 seconds, and breathe out for 5 seconds. Play around with your breathing counts to see what feels right for you.

I first used this above technique when I would get overwhelmed and stressed at work. I found it to be very helpful in regulating my nervous system.

Give yourself time and grace or kindness as you begin to implement these practices in your day.

5. Practice this activity before using the Choose Again Method. Start by being aware of how many negative thoughts you have in a day, and make note of the number. In most cases, it will be shocking. Your thoughts are what create your life around you, so the more positive they are the better you will see them show up in your daily life. It's still important to feel your feelings as they come up, and then let them go floating by you like a cloud or bubble.

6. Use the Choose Again Method. Get in the habit of reaching for a new, more positive thought. Try this for a day and then two days, and so on. The more comfortable you get with shifting your thoughts and your mindset, the better your external life will become. You will also feel happier, and more at peace inside having learned how to focus on so much good all around you. More good or abundance will then be attracted into your current reality.

Unstuck

*"You need to learn to select your thoughts just the same way you select
your clothes every day. There is a power you can cultivate. If you want
to control things in your life so bad, work on your mind. That's the only
thing you should be trying to control."*
—Elizabeth Gilbert

Breaking Old Thought Patterns

It has been ingrained in you to have certain beliefs, conditioning, and stories that you have adopted, which in turn play out in your patterns. At this stage, now that you have looked at reframing your thoughts to shift your mindset, it's time to identify those stories that you tell yourself and beliefs that play over and over again in your life.

I've given you examples of some of my old beliefs and stories that I've had to release in regards to narcissistic managers and relationships that, looking back, so clearly formed a pattern. I'm going to share another belief and story that I told myself for over twenty years. I broke that pattern and discovered that the healing I needed was possible when I finally was ready to write a new story.

We are all made up of energy. We store all of these feelings, which become suppressed emotions in the body. They can manifest or develop into illness or pain over time.

By feeling your feelings as they come up, you release stuck energy in your body.

I had a 20 plus year chronic neck trapezius injury that also affected my back.

I was rear ended in a car accident stopped at a light.

I braced for impact, tensing my entire body as I heard the squealing tires.

I had terrible whiplash and took the brunt of the accident, since only the bumper needed to be replaced on my SUV.

Cars back then didn't have all the features they do now to protect you. I was holding so much trapped energy, emotions and pain in my body from this injury. Over the years, I saw chiropractors and physical therapists and I accepted that I was going to feel pain when my injury flared up, and that no one could fix it.

That's how I lived my life.

This was my story.

This was my belief.

Back in late December 2021, I realized I could write a new story and a new belief erasing the old one.

Then one day, I found a trainer at my gym who said I can fix that injury. I got ready to say no one can, but then I stopped myself. I said, *"Okay. I'll let you take a look. Let's see what you can do."* This trainer was right!

I knew God and the Universe guided me to him, and he was able to fix my injury. I was amazed and very grateful.

I never pictured working with a bodybuilding trainer at my gym, but I knew this was where I was being guided to. I was sure of it.

Trevor kept me from flaring up, which was such a gift. He helped me to develop so much more strength by lifting weights. When he left the gym, I was concerned, but then the next right trainer came in, Aaron, who helped build up my lower body now. When he left, Derek came in, and he was able to truly heal me, giving me the exercises and a long-term plan on how to continue building strength, agility, flexibility, as well as low cardio impact. He gave me a plan to succeed, to maintain my health, and longevity. I was so truly grateful.

Working with these trainers lasted one and a half years and it was an investment in myself and my well- being. When you say yes and invest in you, it can truly be life changing.

In this example above, I was forced to get out of my comfort zone in order to break this pattern and to write a new story. Even after all the evidence I had over the years that my injury couldn't be fixed, I let that go walking forward in faith and trust. I knew in my heart that God and the Universe guided me to the right trainer or trainers who could heal me. I had to let go of trying to rationalize how a bodybuilder trainer would be the right one to begin to work with, and it was one the best decisions I made. To live a life without chronic pain, having healed, is such a miracle.

Be open to the magic that enters your life.

Allow those miracles and blessings to enter even when they don't make sense.

Getting out of your comfort zone to write new stories and break patterns takes vulnerability or transparency.

When you are doing what is familiar, you aren't growing, learning, or taking risks that are necessary to lead you to that beautiful, blessed life towards your destiny.

There has to be discomfort in order to move to the other side of fear. Everything you want in life is on the other side of your comfort zone. The only question is are you brave enough to take that first step or that next step depending on where you are at in your journey?

This is an amazing journey called life, but are you truly living?

I wasn't and was stuck in the familiar for a long time. I was blessed to have the right people push me out of my comfort zone to change my life in the most amazing ways.

I want to be that person for you who helps you see you want more in life, to feel more fulfilled, to reclaim your heart power, to find your voice, step into your highest personal power, and walk forward into your destiny or purpose.

How Do You Get Unstuck?

1. **Try New Things.** This is all about breaking patterns and routines. What does that look like? Sign up or try a new activity, class, take a walk in a new direction, go to a different park, a different grocery store, coffee shop, or restaurant. Try something that you haven't ordered before on the menu, cook a new dish, take a trip, meet new people, strike up a conversation with someone you don't know, try a new hairstyle, new clothing style, work with a trainer, a coach, go out in nature, join a hiking group or walking group, learn to stand up paddle board, take a yoga or spin class, read a new book in a different genre than you are used to. There are so many new things to try all the time. Once you get past your nerves of trying a couple new things, it will become so much more fun, bringing so much more excitement into your life.

2. **Be Open and Vulnerable or Transparent.** When you do something being both brave and scared at the same time, you are moving forward. You are saying, *"I'm setting fear aside and I'm doing this anyway"*. This is all about taking chances and risks to move in a new direction. If you are afraid to speak up at work or to take on a presentation, say yes. It's about saying yes to get unstuck. *"I don't know how to do that, but*

yes I'm willing to learn". If it's something that will help you to learn, and develop a new skill, it may be a good growth opportunity.

3. **Allow Yourself to Be Stretched.** This is about being open to new experiences, people, and adventures to get you out of your comfort zone. It's not about people pleasing here, so be careful. Ask is this an opportunity that will help you to grow that will benefit you. It's not about benefiting anyone else. I've grown the most when I'm stretched into new roles and responsibilities that are far outside of my scope. I built my first website for my business, and I am not technical at all really. I found an online hour tutorial on building a website and I kept rewinding and or pausing as I built my site step by step alongside the video. I grew so much having experienced that growth challenge. The more you grow and realize that you are capable of more than you imagined you will watch your self- confidence build.

4. **Stop Making Excuses.** Stop saying, *"I can't do this. This can't be done. I'm not capable of achieving that level"*, or *"I'm not capable of completing that task"*. Stop saying, *"I shouldn't do that because 1 don't know how to"*. No more excuses! You are capable of anything that you set your mind to. As long as you believe, you can achieve it. Also, stop thinking, *"I'll do it tomorrow, or later"*, and *"I don't feel like it today"*. It's about showing up whether you want to or not. For example, does a writer say, *"I'm only going to write when I'm inspired"*? No, or else we wouldn't have so many books written. It's about showing up to write anyway. Another example is, *"I don't feel like going to the gym"*. Sure, there

are days I feel like that. I remind myself that, if I don't go, it's a slippery slope. I spent so much money, time, energy, and effort to heal my body and to get strong. If I don't go and get off schedule, then my body will hurt, I will be backtracking, and all that effort I and my trainers put in would be wasted if I don't take care of myself.

5. **Take Small Steps.** You don't have to figure it all out at once. Take one small step each day to get unstuck. Get out of your head with overthinking, and instead envision yourself taking one step in front of the other moving forward on your path. For example, today you focused on self-care by making time for a relaxing bath. Be proud of each step you take no matter how small it is. It's still progress when you are moving forward.

6. **Celebrate Small and Big Wins.**

Be your biggest cheerleader.

Celebrate the smallest of wins daily.

For example, *"Yeah! They had my favorite ice cream flavor today. I sat outside and took a few deep breaths while I enjoyed being in nature. I woke up ten minutes early and meditated. I got a good night's sleep. I ate at my favorite restaurant for lunch. I spoke kindly to myself instead of judging. I complimented someone even though that's out of my comfort zone, and that person smiled, saying thank you"*.

Big wins can be anything -- celebrating a promotion, a sale, cooking a new dish that you enjoyed, or planning a vacation. It can be booking a retreat, going to the spa, hiring a fitness trainer, or buying a new car.

It could even be finding a new apartment or house, breaking a pattern, signing up for a new class, making a new friend, or a date that you are excited to go on.

You can 100 percent get out of your comfort zone and choose again at any time.

Say yes to what excites you, intrigues you, feels aligned, and where you are being guided to.

It's important to always listen to your inner guidance, and I'm not suggesting doing anything that is unsafe in a way that could risk your safety.

Use your best judgment to know what is right for you. Your physical safety and well- being is always first and foremost.

Reflection Questions and Actions:

1. Can you recall a similar story in your life to mine where you have a belief that is holding you back from achieving what you desire or keeping you stuck?

2. What is that belief that is keeping you stuck? How can you shift your mindset to create a new belief and story to get unstuck?

3. **Ask yourself how often are you:**

   a. **Trying New things – How** often? What have you tried? What do you want to try that you haven't yet?

   b. **Being Open and Vulnerable, Transparent** – How often?
   What have you done to be open and transparent?
   What else could you be doing to be more open and transparent?

   c. **Allowing Yourself to Be Stretched** –How often?

What have you done to allow yourself to be stretched more day to day?

What else could you be doing to allow yourself more opportunities to grow and or be stretched?

d. **Stop Making Excuses** – Are you making excuses? How often?

What are the stories and thoughts you tell yourself?

e. **Taking Small Steps** – Are you taking small steps each day to move forward in life? What small steps have you taken?

What small steps could you be taking to move towards what has been put on your heart, what you truly desire?

f. **Celebrate Small and Big Wins** – Are you celebrating your wins? Big? Small? How often? What wins have you been celebrating? List them out, especially your small every day wins.

Learning How to Be Vulnerable or Transparent

Being vulnerable definitely made me uncomfortable.

I also use transparent because I feel it to be a safer, more comfortable word. Through a great deal of my healing, I was taught to be vulnerable, so that is the word that connects best for me.

Being vulnerable isn't weak as you may often have thought.

Being emotional means that you are connecting with your feelings, and should lose the negative connotation.

In my opinion, feeling and being connected to what comes up for you is healthy. You have been taught to bury your feelings and anything that comes up. *"Well, I don't want to feel that. I don't want to go there again or open that door"*.

Those feelings and emotions that resurfaced get stuffed back down again, which is a missed opportunity to heal.

Next time those feelings or emotions bubble up, revisit them, let them in, saying, *"I'm curious and want to understand more"*.

Find out where they are coming from by sitting in your vulnerability or transparency, instead of running from them.

Ask why they are coming up now. Pay attention to the response you receive.

Allow yourself to be in the moment, feeling it all. It can be so healing when you feel what is coming up, and sit in those feelings for a short time. Then, visualize where in your body those feelings are leaving from, and watch them float away passing right above you, and then out of sight.

I'm going to share a time in my life where I first learned to be vulnerable or transparent, and how it greatly impacted my life in a positive way. This is when I was fairly new to healing. I already had learned how to feel my feelings before this stage, and this was the next big step that I was ready to take in my healing journey to connect with the true me.

Brené Brown's The Gift of Imperfection

At 34 years old, I was so blessed to have a coach come into my life who changed my world in the most powerful, yet beautiful ways. The more vulnerable or transparent I became, the more I realized I was outgrowing the ego that was trying to keep me safe and stuck in life.

My relationship coach, Lisa, who I worked with over a decade ago, introduced me to Brené Brown's book, *The Gift of Imperfection*, which was a game changer for me. There are so many valuable messages in this book.

You only truly hear the messages that you are ready for. Think of it this way. You may have watched a movie five years ago, and then one day you decide to watch it again. All of a sudden, you are connecting with all these messages and words that you didn't even hear back then.

You weren't ready to understand those messages at the time, but now you are.

You see things through your own perspective or lens based on the experiences you've had in your own life. Ever get frustrated and wonder why someone can't understand where you are coming from? It seems so clear and logical to you.

Each person sees things through their own lens, from the experiences that shaped them.

The Gift of Imperfection: Four Key Takeaways

Brené Brown's book helped me understand how to change my life.

She showed me that the gift is in being imperfect, and that you aren't supposed to be perfect. It's all about letting go of the shame and discovering who you are, showing up as the real you without a mask. It's okay to be in your messiness and embrace it.

Let go of this need to please everyone around you trying to be perfect. At the time I first read this book, I received four key takeaways. It amazes me to go back through it so many years later realizing so many other topics in how I live my life and coach clients didn't even register back then. I don't even remember reading them because I wasn't ready to understand yet.

- **The First Key Takeaway: Be Vulnerable** – Brené Brown talked about the importance of vulnerability, and that you just might have to take that action or do that thing when you are brave and scared at the same time. My coach pushed me to be vulnerable, opening up my heart, and no longer playing

84

it safe. It was about being brave even when I was afraid, and taking that action anyway. She wanted me to tell a guy I liked him. I was scared after we had a few really good dates when he sent a message saying that he wasn't ready to date. She taught me how to express my feelings, and that it wasn't about the outcome. All that mattered is that I spoke up being open and vulnerable. This tied into the second key takeaway, which was getting out of my comfort zone.

- **The Second Key Takeaway: Get Out of Your Comfort Zone** – Doing things that would get me unstuck even though I was afraid to do them actually turned out to make me feel really good. I loved the excitement of living life and not being a bystander. It was scary to get out of my comfort zone. There was always constant change in the Medical Sales Industry, working for a big corporation, so outside of work, I wanted to be in the familiar. This was an adjustment for me for sure, and it was definitely worth it. Everything you want in life comes from the other side of your comfort zone. Once you begin to take steps and see how much good comes from getting out of your comfort zone, it will become easier to keep taking those steps forward each day. The third key takeaway was around shame.

- **The Third Key Takeaway: Overcome Shame** – I didn't even know what shame was back then. Brené Brown said that each of us has shame. It's what keeps us from feeling worthy to do great things in life. We think, "*How can I do that? Will she do it better than me? There are all these other women doing that already, how can I? I'm not meant to be* *seen, who would listen to me?"* – The fourth key takeaway was you have to love yourself.

- **The Fourth Key Takeaway: Love Yourself** – That love you seek is within you. You need to love yourself to feel worthy of what you want in life. I quickly came to understand that I was so hard on myself because I didn't love myself and I lacked self-esteem, which is why, at first, I saw myself as a victim from being in that long term narcissistic, emotionally abusive relationship. Very quickly, I shifted my mindset to realize that I was being a gift here with this coach. It was time to receive help to learn how to love myself and develop a healthy self-esteem.

Reflection Questions and Actions:

1. How can you be more vulnerable or transparent to get out of your comfort zone?
2. Can you think of a time when you watched a movie or heard a message picking up on it later in life when you were ready and it surprised you that it didn't resonate the first time around? What happened in this situation? Do you remember what you first heard? Then later the message that resonated when you were ready to hear it?
3. Looking at the Four Key Takeaways I learned from Brené's book where do you sit on a scale of 1-5, 5 being the highest. Do you see yourself as being vulnerable 1-5, Are you living outside of your comfort zone 1-5, Do you feel like you are impacted by shame of not being enough 1-5? On a scale of 1-5, How much do you love yourself?

    ____ Being Vulnerable or Transparent?

___ Getting out of your Comfort Zone?

___ Feeling Shame?

___ Loving Yourself?

Removing the Triggers

"Above all, be the heroine of your life, not the victim."
—*Nora Ephron*

Let's review why inner healing work is so important. The more you heal, the healthier all of your relationships will be, including the one with yourself.

Healing will help you get to know the true you, the essence of your soul deep within. When you do the healing work, you will connect with your heart power, grow your self -love and find your voice as you step into your highest personal power, a more fulfilled life while walking into what you are here to do in this world.

Healing is necessary to allow you to grow, learn, clearing out all the programming or old conditioning, outdated stories, and beliefs that no longer resonate.

I'm going to walk you through some of the inner healing work I did, releasing trauma from being picked on as a kid that followed me for so very many years. Learning to love my inner child grew my self- love so much.

Each of you has an inner child. She is the child within you who comes out when you are having fun, get excited, get upset, become scared, or are really happy. She is so often forgotten about and buried when the busyness of life gets in the way. By getting to know her and allowing her to be a part of you again, you will be able to heal further, as well as open your heart like you did as a child.

The time came for my first online session with the relationship coach, Lisa. Right away, she told me that I had to hold myself accountable. I chose this relationship, and I'm not the victim here. Then she shared that I had self- esteem issues, which was why I had been in that relationship. *"Wow! Kick me when I'm down"*, I thought.

I had just been treated badly, spoken to harshly, and now this relationship coach is saying this to me. I reflected on what she said, trying to take my emotions out of it. It was really hard and painful to hear, but I knew I needed to hear it. I realized that this was the moment that I was ready to hear the hard, painful reality of my part in all of it. I knew she was right, as much as I didn't want to hear or admit that.

Lisa was such a gift to me. She was a blessing who forced me to see the reality of my life and she helped me to change it.

We did a lot of deep healing work, getting into my childhood trauma of where this all stemmed from. I knew a lot of why I made the choices I did already. Even at twenty-six years old, sitting with the therapist, I could already tell her so much of what I understood about me and where all my issues stemmed from. That saved time in this case, too.

Lisa had healing abilities that I didn't realize at the time, but have after my Spiritual Awakening. God brought her to me to heal my inner child, setting me forward on a path to walk towards my destiny. I had deep childhood trauma from being picked on as a child by the girls at school. This is where so much of the lack of self-worth, self-confidence, and self-love came from.

I hated my inner child, the little girl within me. She is the child in you that comes out when you are scared, angry, sad, hard on yourself, shaming or blaming yourself, feeling guilty, or not feeling good enough. That is where you will find her.

She needs to feel safe, loved, and always protected.

She is such a beautiful part of you.

All she wants is to be heard, seen, loved, and cared for.

I was so mean to my inner child. I blamed her for everything that ever happened to me, saying *"It's all your fault"*. Up to that point I spent my entire life being hard on that little girl within me. I hated her and told her that all the time.

Lisa showed me that I needed to learn to love her and that she was a special part of me. I then was able to change the way I spoke to her. Every day I would tell her I love her. I would allow her to be a bigger part of my life.

Over the years, I learned to check in with her, asking what she wants to do today.

I ask what would make her feel safe and protected.

I take her to watch the butterflies and dragonflies dance around in the park by me because it makes her so happy.

I give her ice cream when she wants a treat.

When you connect with your inner child, there is more of a feeling of being whole as you reconnect with the child within you. Take her hand and show her the way as you would a child, helping her to feel safe and loved.

The inner child does not like change. It makes her feel very unsafe. When you have big changes in your life, make sure that she knows just how much she is loved. If you feel anxiety come on, it's most likely your inner child panicking.

Connect with her, find out how she is feeling, and most importantly honor her feelings.

Do not judge her in any way. She is allowed to feel her feelings. Just remember that she is still that child. She doesn't have all the life experience that you do, and will still see everything through her child-like lens or filter.

Get to know her, find out her age, what she wants from you, and how you can work together to live in harmony.

She is such a beautiful part of you, and deserves to be seen, too.

She is your playful, fun side who doesn't always come out, especially when you are so focused on the demands of this busy life that you have created.

Reflection Questions and Actions:

Inner Child:

It's important to get to know your inner child, reconnecting with her, before you can help her to heal.

1. How old do you see your inner-child?
2. List 5 things the child in you gets excited about, puts a smile on your face, makes her truly happy, and loves to do? These can be activities. Mine loves to color, loves kid's movies, watching the butterflies and dragonflies dance around, loves ice cream, running across the field in the park with my little dog, chasing my little dog Chloe around, and watching The new version of The Little Mermaid, singing along.
3. What are some "treats" she loves? (These don't have to be edible but could include smells, sounds, or tactile experiences).
4. Aside from connecting with and taking care of your inner child, what else can you do to help her heal?

Trigger Work to Heal:

1. Besides inner child healing work, what else can you do? Pay attention to your triggers and look for patterns.

2. What is triggering you? When are you being triggered? Who are you around when you are being triggered? Is there a common thread or pattern of something that is triggering you? What feelings are coming up for you when you are being triggered?

3. Write these answers down in a journal or on the phone under reminders or the notes section, so that you can be a detective finding a link or pattern.

Welcome your triggers, invite them in, and say thank you for showing me that there are areas that need healing. Once you learn how to do this healing work, you will be able to manage your triggers quickly as they come up in the future. The more healing work you do, the less scary it will be.

Like I've said, healing will help you in all areas of your life, and in all of your relationships, including the one with you. In my experience, it is so worth doing the inner healing work to finally meet the true you underneath all the cloudiness from the outside world. This is truly the greatest gift that you could ever give yourself. Aren't you worth it?

As you heal, you will clear out old programming or conditioning, previous patterns, and outdated stories, as well as past beliefs. I'll go much more in depth in this area further in this book.

You will understand how logical this spiritual journey of growth and walking into your destiny really is. It will begin to make sense what you are here for and the meaning of life.

Healing will allow you to connect fully with your own heart as you claim your heart power.

Healing will grow your self-love and self-worth.

Healing will build your confidence.

Healing helps you to feel more fulfilled.

Healing is the most powerful experience you can give yourself. It is a gift that you can benefit from the rest of your life as well as those around you.

Your healing will inspire so many other women to do the same thing. You will show all those around you that they are worth it, as they find their voice, and stand in their highest personal power, sharing all of them with the world as God intended.

Opening Your Heart

"Courage starts with showing up and letting ourselves be seen."
—Brené Brown

I realized that I needed help. It was time for me to admit that I clearly have no idea what to do when it comes to dating.

COVID helped me to realize that I wanted more in life. I decided that I wanted to find my person, true love, and that life would be more meaningful with love. I was ready to put myself out there and try again.

I loved myself, had been learning to set boundaries, stopped people pleasing for the most part, and I was feeling good about who I had become, and what I brought to the table in a relationship. I had been spending years working on myself, and now it was time to try something new, totally out of my comfort zone, signing up to work with a husband-and-wife relationship coach team.

They taught me so much and helped me to meet quality men online who took me out on good dates. I began to shift my mindset to enjoying the process of dating. They taught me the right questions to ask to get conversations going even in text messages. I learned how to weed out the guys who were not going to make the effort, and or were not really interested in getting into a relationship. They helped me share who I was in my profile, so that I shined bright as the true me.

It didn't take long at all to get in a relationship.

Within a couple of weeks, I had met a great guy. We clicked on the first date, the conversation flowed, and we were instantly comfortable with each other.

Shortly after, I was in an exclusive relationship with this man.

I remember on my birthday, less than two months after we met, he showed up with a dozen red roses, and took me out to a nice dinner.

I felt so special, and wasn't used to being treated so well. This was a much healthier relationship than I had been in before.

This was new territory for me, and I was happy to walk down this road. Fast forward to October 2021, and we took a romantic trip to Paris. It was still during COVID, but the airlines just opened back up, so it all worked out. I was grateful to go! Having to wear a face mask the majority of the time from California to Paris was worth it.

As I lay next to my boyfriend in Paris, I thought to myself, "I'm *the luckiest girl in the world*". Even in the moment that I wasn't feeling well, having indulged in too much French food that night, and unable to sleep with the time change, I felt so grateful.

Here I was with a caring, loving man who was gently touching my upper forehead, brushing my hair back with his hand to help me relax, so that I would fall asleep.

I had never experienced this before. "*Is this what one would call a healthy, loving relationship*," I asked myself. I was embracing all of this.

We were so comfortable together after 3.5 months having taken a vacation to Paris together. I had spent time with his family already and he had met mine as well. Kind of important when you are going to travel around the world with someone.

I loved feeling like a mom to his four-year-old daughter. I felt more joy than I had ever felt before, spending time with this little girl who was so imaginative and full of life. It began to wake up something in me as I saw the world through a child's eyes. The world she created was filled with so much magic and wonder. I loved being a part of it all.

Back to Paris – even though my boyfriend woke up with his ankle all swollen, he still insisted on walking throughout the city uphill in pain. I was so supportive of him all day, suggesting we take a cab, but he insisted on walking because he really wanted to share that special part of Paris with me on foot. I even said that it's okay if we don't go. You don't want to injure your foot more when you are training for a marathon.

That evening, we had a romantic picnic by the Seine where he got up the nerve to tell me he loved me. Then, to my surprise, he told me that he was head over heels in love with me. That was the first time I had ever heard anyone say, "*I'm in love with you*", never mind "*I'm head over heels in love with you.*" At that moment, my heart was so filled with joy.

It was then that my heart opened. I felt the exact same way. I heard I love you and I'm in love with you more times than I have my entire life all together. This was an entirely new experience for me as I didn't even know how to be in love.

Words poured from my heart, so profound and beautiful that I didn't even know where they came from. This part of my heart that was under lock and key was finally opened for the first time. I felt alive and so much love, but also so much anxiety.

It was at this time a few weeks later that my boyfriend started to panic with the holidays coming. All of a sudden, everything was too real and overwhelming for him. Fear of upsetting his teenage daughters from his first marriage set in. What if he got it wrong again, a third time, he asked himself. He couldn't do that to his kids.

I didn't understand why, at 4.5 months, he was already trying to figure out if we would make it to the altar. He got so in his head and I got really scared as he began to pull away and shut down.

I called my relationship coach in a panic asking for help. I wanted to fix this relationship and go back to how amazing things were just a few short weeks ago. I knew that Jeff was putting way too much pressure on himself, me, and us. Instead of enjoying each moment together, he was trying to figure it all out, jumping ahead into the future.

My coach told me that he would help me, and we even got Jeff to join us on a call to hear his perspective and how he was feeling. I felt good knowing that my coach knew what to do in this situation, and I felt reassured. He then proceeded to teach me how to live in my authenticity. I had no idea what this term even meant at that time. I was so far out of my comfort zone, and was willing to do whatever it took to fix this relationship, making it better.

What does living in your authenticity even mean? Don't we all wear masks until you feel safe to take your mask off? Isn't that "normal"?

Allowing someone to see only parts of you at a time was normal to me, and I thought that everyone lived this way. I'd heard this in the past so many times.

Don't share too much in a text, leave some mystery.

Don't share your whole life story with someone. It should only be pieces at a time.

You may be asking yourself, "*How am I ever going to be able to live in my authenticity?*" Trust me I asked the same question and, when the time was right, I did just that.

It didn't mean that I felt ready to, but I knew that I was supposed to, and it was 100 percent necessary to move me forward to where I was meant to be. I can't really explain it, except that I had this *knowing*, and

I trusted my relationship coach in 2021 as he was showing me how to do this.

First of all, I had no idea how to live in my authenticity.

My coach had to explain this concept to me in a way that made sense. After having a call with both Jeff and I, he told me that I needed to open up, sharing more of who I was. That was what Jeff needed from me to connect more emotionally.

I asked my coach for some examples because I really didn't know how to share more of myself with a boyfriend.

My heart had been very guarded for a long time, and I was now taking the walls down, which was terrifying.

Let's call it like it is.

I was told examples of questions, such as sharing your philosophy on life, share when you were the happiest in your life, and why.

Deep thought-provoking questions were what he was getting at, to really get to know each other at a more emotionally intimate level.

He also told me to switch it up. One week be more loving, sharing my heartfelt emotions I felt for Jeff. Then, the next week, I needed to make it more fun and playful. The week after that, he wanted me to ask more deep level, connective, bonding questions.

My coach told me to keep opening up and that I had to show all of me, fully leaning in.

I didn't want to, but I knew I was supposed to continue forward completely outside of my comfort zone.

I was so anxious all the time waiting to see how this would all turn out.

I shared all of me, even though it was so scary to put my heart on the line.

As uncomfortable as it was for me, I opened up to Jeff. I shared the story of being picked on as a kid by the girls for so many years, being nicknamed Queen Baldy the Third because I have fine hair. Looking back at pictures, I looked like the other kids. There really weren't any physical differences. It was because I wanted to be liked and to fit in with the girls so badly that I made an easy mark. I had plenty of hair, and that nickname was really pretty silly, but as a kid it traumatized me for a long time. I always believed that I was different and that there was something wrong with me.

Jeff was supportive when I poured my heart out, tears streaming down my face.

He gave me a hug and asked some questions to understand more, which showed he cared.

At the time, I didn't realize that my coach was making this about my growth whether or not things worked out with my boyfriend.

I was becoming a new person. I was about to awaken to living an entirely new way with a life full of purpose and meaning.

I continued to pour my heart out living in my authenticity, which I had just discovered. No more hiding parts of me.

The most vulnerable moments in my life were exposed as I shared all of me.

As I opened up sharing all of me in the most vulnerable of ways, Jeff put his walls back up. Even though Jeff had asked to connect at a more emotionally deep level in our relationship, it showed him that he had more healing work and growing to do. Although he didn't realize this yet.

Even when Jeff broke up with me a month later, the week before Christmas, I knew that it was happening for a reason. I trusted that there was a gift in here somewhere. He wasn't healed enough after his second marriage ended, and I realized how much work he still had to do during the breakup. God gave me the words he needed to hear as I dried my tears. I didn't even know I was channeling at the time, but those months were the beginning of my gifts opening as my heart did. I shared with him the healing work that he still needed to do connecting the dots of what was going on internally for him.

I call this relationship a close one. It wasn't right for either of us. Rejection is protection, right? It showed me some of what I wanted in the right person.

The breakup was tough.

I was so attached to his youngest daughter, and that was incredibly painful for me. She was very attached too, always jumping in my arms, sometimes calling me mommy by accident as I read her a bedtime story. It turned out that I had more growing to do in order to be ready for the right one.

God has been preparing me ever since the end of 2021. He has shown me that I deserve consistency, not intensity. Someone who is steady, no rush, stable, where you are sure of each other.

I know that is what I deserve and it will happen all in perfect, right, divine timing.

Through this relationship, I opened up my whole heart at a level I had never experienced. Being authentic is scary, but it was absolutely worth it. I shared my childhood trauma of being mercilessly picked on by the girls at school as tears streamed down my face. I felt anxiety all the time as I opened my heart more and more to him and not realizing in that moment, to myself.

I thought opening up was to make our relationship better, to save it, but in reality, it was about me sharing who I truly was. I was so fearful of this man I loved leaving me. The gift was in connecting with myself, getting out of my comfort zone, and opening my heart. I was so blessed to have an amazing relationship coach who taught me so much, walking me through all the steps I needed to take to open my heart fully coming back to who I truly was deep inside. I will always be so grateful for him as he helped me to walk forward, awakening to a beautiful and blessed life–One where I found fulfillment.

My relationship coach was super supportive of me through the breakup. He wanted me to process my feelings, get crystal clear on what I wanted, and create a list of the qualities I want in the right person.

Also, get clear on the qualities that were not the right fit in this relationship that just ended.

I made my lists. I journaled to get all my feelings and thoughts out of my head as well.

Two friends recommended I do journaling, and one said, "*I bet it's tiring to have that mental chatter running through your head non-stop*". They were both right. I didn't know how therapeutic journaling could be, but it really is.

I found that, every time I had all these thoughts and feelings in my head from the breakup during the day, I would write them all down. I felt much calmer doing this.

My coach gave me some powerful advice when I was ready. He said, "Dip in and out of your grief. Don't make it your home or camp there." I took this to heart and I followed it. Later, I understood why he said this.

I knew I was supposed to keep my heart open, so I did whatever it would take to stay in my heart. I shared my feelings with everyone I knew, being vulnerable to keep my heart open. Any time someone who loved me put Jeff down in any way, I focused on the good. You know the typical you deserve better, and how could he break up with you a week before Christmas. His life is way too intense and chaotic. You don't need to deal with all of that. I knew we weren't right for each other, but I still wanted to honor him and the relationship.

I spent time going to the gym, trying an intro to kettlebell class, which is where I met that first trainer who was able to heal my old auto injury from more than twenty years ago. I kept getting out of my comfort zone knowing that I was being guided somewhere new.

I didn't understand it just yet, but I was about to.

I attended my friend's church, and I hadn't seen her in three years.

The pieces were about to start to come together.

I cried on and off for a couple of weeks, and once I got to January 2, 2022, I started feeling better. I even shared with my relationship group what happened, and they saw me as brave for sharing my heart. I thought I would be seen as a failure.

"Maybe there was something to being vulnerable," I thought.

Staying vulnerable or transparent is what was keeping my heart to stay open. I started creating a whole new life that new year.

I said yes to all new things, experiences, and people, and in that I connected more with who I truly was.

I let go of fear in trying new things and meeting all these people I didn't know realizing it was time for some huge life changes.

I joined Gabby's Miracle Membership at this time and started coaching at Singles Ministry at the new church I was attending.

I jumped head first into the deep end of my Spirituality online.

I ended up meeting so many amazing people.

I had awakened to a new reality – I was going through a rebirth as I was becoming all of me underneath all the old conditioning, outdated stories, and old beliefs.

I was choosing again, doing things differently.

Having broken so many of my patterns, I walked into a whole new way of living.

When I refer to a rebirth or death in this book, I mean you go through different seasons in life where you grow into an entirely new person. You shed old parts that die off and no longer resonate. I just want to clarify in case you were wondering what I mean here.

I let go as some would say so much of what was holding me back, keeping me stuck, and I leapt forward to a beautiful new beginning.

When you get out of your comfort zone, break old patterns by writing new stories, choosing again, you in turn end up with a different outcome where your life will change in the most amazing ways. You will move forward to creating the life that you truly desire, one that is fulfilling that your heart and soul are guiding you to.

In my experience, inner healing work, all of the growth experiences both the fun, good ones and the painful ones are all necessary to move you forward in your journey.

Choose to take a step forward each day. You don't have to change everything at once. I know that my Spiritual Awakening allowed me to propel forward so rapidly because ultimately, I was ready.

Life is about soul expansion. I had been taking so many steps over the years to expand and grow, that one day, the time came and I took that huge leap, truly believing that there was more meaning to life, and I was blessed to have found that summer of 2023, stepping into my soul mission.

Focus on your growth the way you do on other aspects of your life, and you will end up here at the right time for you. You are truly a work of art underneath it all.

Get curious about the woman deep inside you. She can't wait to meet you. You are getting closer every day to meeting the true you, and you are absolutely worth it.

Reflection Questions and Actions:

You can take small steps every day to live in your authenticity. Start getting real with yourself.

1. Ask yourself what areas are you stuck in? Where do you need help?

Don't be afraid to ask for help. I believe everyone can benefit from help. I had to admit I needed help with dating because I wasn't getting it right after all these years. That's what brought me originally to my relationship coach in 2021. I ended up doing group and one on one coaching with him, and my entire life changed in ways I could have never imagined. I had to say yes to me, investing in myself, saying I'm worth it. I didn't know any women in my life at the time who were investing in themselves to grow, and evolve, trying something new, getting out of their comfort zone. I had to be the first.

2. Ask these questions again:
    a. Say yes to you. How can you start to invest in yourself today?
    b. Get honest about what areas you want to change in your life?

3. Choose a moment where you stand up for yourself. You could speak up when you want to go to a particular restaurant. Share what it is that you feel like doing instead of people pleasing, or going along with what everyone else wants to do.

4. Start to commit to speaking your truth, sharing something important to you a few days a week, and it will get easier. Tell yourself

this is important to me, I'm sharing the real me, and if people don't like the real me it's time to make some new friends or be open to making the necessary changes in my life.

Forging Forgiveness

"Forgiveness is really a gift to yourself – have the compassion to forgive others, and the courage to forgive yourself."
—Mary Anne Radmacher

Forgiveness Will Allow You to Heal

Forgiveness is imperative in your healing journey. All that you want is on the other side of fear. When you are angry and hurt, so much of that is connected to your Ego, and from a place of fear. To truly forgive is to see someone and a situation out of love. That narcissistic ex of yours was cruel, hurt you, belittled you, caused you to cry endless tears, and you probably feel angry and hurt that he tricked you. He lured you in with his adoration, and then turned on you.

After experiencing such abuse, you are probably still angry with yourself for staying as long as you did, maybe for exposing your kids to his behavior for so many years.

Now is the time in your healing journey to forgive yourself. I mean forgive at a deep level, letting go of the anger and at the same time forgiving your emotional abuser. I know this is really hard to do, but for me and my clients it has been life changing. It will take so much weight off your shoulders and will help to soften your heart. You can only do what you are ready for, so keep an open mind as you read this chapter following the exercises. It may be necessary to come back to forgiveness at another time.

Honor yourself and where you are at, making sure to give yourself so much grace, kindness, and compassion. This is a judgment free space.

Forgiving My Emotional Abuser and Myself

I buried all my pain after my emotionally abusive relationship that ended over a decade ago. I didn't even know that I had trauma that wasn't healed. I just thought that I got over it as enough time passed by. I realized that I never really forgave my ex- boyfriend Greg. I saw it as a gift shortly after I walked away having worked with Lisa, my relationship coach. That painful relationship was the catalyst for healing my inner child, working on my self-esteem issues, and learning to love myself.

In January 2022, I joined Gabby Bernstein's Miracle Member Group, and at the same time I was ready to reread her book *Super Attractor*. I started using her affirmation cards as well, to know what I needed.

I remember driving across the Bay Bridge in San Francisco for work one day, and I said out loud, *I forgive you Greg.* I realized in that moment, after all these years, that was the first time I had truly forgiven him. I wished him peace too and hoped that he was well. It was powerful to see that I wasn't holding that anger or hurt anymore.

Then, in Spring 2022, I was driving in San Francisco, going to visit one of the hospitals for work, and I was detoured right through the area we used to live. I felt fear wash over me as I gripped the wheel so tightly my hands hurt. At that moment, I pictured him as a little boy and I pictured me as a little girl. I said, *I forgive you. You were scared, and afraid to open up again after your wife left you. You were hurting, and didn't want to let me in. You were doing the best that you could at the time.* I thought after these two experiences that I had done enough deep healing work to have freed myself of any triggers. I was wrong.

A Valuable, Yet Painful Gift

God gave me a valuable, yet painful gift in the summer of 2023. As I was alone for three days with who I believed could be my person, far from home, having followed God's guidance, I came face to face with who I would consider to be a narcissist. This was a gift because it gave me the opportunity to heal at a deeper level. I was triggered in ways I wasn't prepared for.

Reliving my past moments of being questioned, judged, belittled, never saying the right thing, literally feeling like I was going crazy. I felt all these emotions that were once buried bubble to the surface as I felt so much anxiety. I was reliving my pain at the same time as experiencing it all over again with this man. The one who I believed God brought into my life to love and adore me.

Once it became real and we met, for some reason it didn't feel right. Something was missing. He wasn't that cruel narcissist type I had encountered before with a cold disposition. Instead, he was holding himself accountable over the months we got to know each other long distance. I was in complete shock as I didn't know who was standing in front of me. I knew that God had his reasons, and that this was going to help me rise to where he wanted me to be. In that moment, all I felt was pain as I relived and replayed in person how more than one ex - boyfriend of mine treated me. I flashed back the most to my long -term relationship with Greg, where the most damage had been done.

Powerful Realizations, Connecting the Dots

I also flashed to a friend of mine who I dated back in 2013/2014. We were close and we had a wonderful romantic trip where I felt so loved, taken care of, and protected. He came to visit me and met some of my friends. No red flags. We were close and completely trusted one another, or so I thought. One of the trips where I visited him, everything changed.

He was majorly triggered by something I said, and he completely shut down. It was so innocent to me. I said that it was up to him if we should stay and watch the rest of the game or we could go. I agreed with him that his team wasn't playing well, but that I was good either way. He said I was being passive aggressive, and for the rest of the night he was cold towards me.

This kind, loving man, who everyone thought the world of, including me, ignored my crying with tears streaming down my face all night. It felt terrible. He had opened up so much to me and shared so much of who he was, what he believed in, letting me into his world. Now, I'm far from home and I felt so alone. He apologized the next morning, feeling terrible for how he behaved. I cried to a friend that day when he was at work, and she said he probably wasn't over his ex-wife yet, and his past relationship after that.

I ended up having him take me to where my friend was, and I stayed with her and her mother for the duration of my trip. I decided that I shouldn't meet his family after everything that happened. I didn't understand at the time until I was on my trip with the man God brought me to fast forward to summer of 2023 again.

I saw similar behavior, and in that moment, I believed my friend all those years ago was exhibiting clear narcissistic behavior.

I was shocked, but at the same time, it all made so much sense.

I had walked away from what I would refer to as my narcissistic, emotionally abusive relationship all those years ago, met someone shortly after him who exhibited the same signs, which I saw really early on having learned my lesson.

Then, I ended up in the situation with my friend who I walked away from, too.

Why then was I being tested with this man God led me to having to learn this lesson yet again?

The Gift in the Lesson

This was a chance to master my lesson, and graduate with flying colors never to repeat this lesson again.

It was a gift as I've explained to heal a deeper part of me, so that I can do my soul mission work that God has called me to do.

It helps me relate and connect more as I just went through recent narcissistic abuse.

It fires me up to help women heal after narcissistic abuse.

I was blessed to have a quick lesson in only three days having met in person.

The rest was months of conversations, practically daily Facetime videos or audio calls, deep conversations, lots of laughs, and what felt like building a beautiful, loving connection. Even on my trip home, God made it crystal clear that this relationship wasn't for me, and that he had other plans. My Uber driver said, *"God told me to tell you not to give this guy another chance. He is going to apologize and ask you to take him back. He will never be healed enough to be with you, and you deserve to be with a man who will truly love you, respect, and support you."*

I had other people I didn't know share similar messages as I was moved to different flights to get home due to weather delays. I was told *that you will never rise to where God wants you if you allow this man back into your life. He will distract you.*

I heard countless similar messages from people. On one flight, I had a sixteen-month-old baby on her mom's lap pointing at me saying *be happy, happy, happy.*

The signs and messages I needed to hear were all around me.

Forgiving Myself and This Man I Cared Deeply For

I was hurt after this experience, even though I saw it as a blessing. In order to rise to where God wanted me, I had to forgive this man and myself. I was so surprised that I didn't see it coming. I missed the subtle signs. God unmasked him in person and I saw so clearly.

All of a sudden, these very subtle signs pieced together and I realized who this man truly was. A man who I wished the best for, but was not for me. For weeks, God would have conversations with me to make sure that I understood the lessons in this experience. I kept asking, *"How could I not see it before after months of endless conversations"*? I was being hard on myself. I had to let go of questioning myself and just focus on this being a gift that I had to open for many reasons.

I saw the good in him, and it was hard to be fooled. For a while, I said I sent him well wishes, but I no longer respect him, which was being real with where I was at. I would ask close spiritual friends and women in the Facebook group I created if that was okay. I wanted confirmation that the way I felt was okay. I hadn't wanted or needed that hardly since my Spiritual Awakening.

My sense of knowing kicked in, realizing that it was time to let go, to truly forgive with all of my heart. That's just what I did. I forgave myself at the same time. It wasn't easy, but that is what I needed to heal at a deeper level, and to say God," *I want to focus on the amazing, loving man, who will respect, support, and cherish me as I know he is on the way shortly."* That is who I deserve and it's time to move forward to where God wants me as I step into my soul mission, my calling, my purpose.

Let's do a visualization exercise.

If you have been sexually or physically abused, please refrain from this visualization and consult a professional therapist or psychologist who is licensed to assist with healing your trauma.

Visualization exercise: Close your eyes and I want you to open the door to a time that immediately comes to you where you feel hurt and angry. Where are you? Picture what is around you and who. How do you feel in this moment going back in as the observer? Note that you are not reliving this experience, and in fact are safe. What feelings are coming up for you? List them out in your head or write them down. Now I want you to put all of those feelings and emotions that have resurfaced in a box.

Picture yourself opening a box, and one by one picture each of these feelings and emotions that you are ready to let go of, that have been weighing you down into this box. Once you have completed this feel the weight in your body lessen. Now what do you want to do with the box? You are walking with this box, and you have the power to decide where to take it. Do you want to throw it in the dumpster outside? Do you want to put it on a shelf in the garage, how high up? Do you want to place it in the kitchen trash? Outside of your front door? Bury it in the dirt? How deep? Do you want to burn the box by having a bonfire? It is your choice to take this box anywhere you want to. I'm just giving you some options.

Now that the box is gone, and you are no longer holding it, how do you feel? Do you feel lighter, and more free? Know that whatever your experience is will be right for you. Feel free to come back and do this visualization further into your healing or at any time you are called to.

Reflection Questions and Actions:

1. As you are further in this book now ask yourself, *"Who do I still need to forgive? Have I truly forgiven myself? Who else needs my forgiveness?"*

It's about you. Forgiving only helps you get unstuck, opens your heart more, and walks you forward towards a beautiful, blessed life. The deeper you go in forgiving where your trauma lies, the better you will feel, connecting to your heart. Love will literally heal you.

2. Forgiveness will lead to a softening of your heart. Write a letter forgiving yourself.

3. Write a letter forgiving the person or persons who hurt you.

4. Some of you have moved on, and found a much healthier relationship. Ask yourself again, have I really let this man into my heart? Do I still have walls up? What can I do to let this person in more?

5. As we have delved deeper into forgiveness, now ask yourself, *"How can I take more of my walls down to bring more of who I am to the surface?"*

Listening to Your Personal Power

"Know what sparks the light in you. Then use that light to illuminate the world."
—Oprah Winfrey

Learning to Follow Your Intuition

How exciting! It's time to start listening to your personal power!

In order to connect to your personal power, you must first learn how to listen and follow your intuition. You may be sitting here thinking how on earth am I going to learn how to do that? Trust me, I understand. So much of this journey to reclaim your heart is about keeping an open mind, letting go of judgment, and feeling your way instead of always thinking. Connecting with your soul whose whispers may be getting louder as you relearn who you truly are under all the old conditioning, outdated stories, and past beliefs.

Think of your intuition as a compass pointing you in the right direction. For example, your intuition is going to get you on the right flight, bus, subway train, or even Uber. There are subtle messages everywhere that are meant for you. When you realize, like I did that, I was meant to end up with that Uber driver who gave me the message I needed to hear, and, I was meant to have my flights changed, so that baby could cheer me up, and that everything is always happening for you, not to you. This is when your world will truly change.

I learned to grow my faith and trust by learning to listen to my intuition. All day, I see signs that I'm where I'm meant to be. It took me time to get here, but I've realized that I never have to worry about when I need to leave the house because I know I will always arrive at my destination at the right moment.

What I mean by this is that I'm connected to that internal compass, so I don't panic if I forget my sunglasses and have to run back in the house because I'm being aligned to the signs and messages I'm meant to see.

When you slow down and are present in this very moment, you will see the guidance around you. All of a sudden, you get this feeling of *"I'm supposed to stop at this store, restaurant, or coffee shop. There is a reason for this"*. The more you begin to connect within, quieting your mind, the easier it will be to feel, hear, or know where and when you should be somewhere in a given day.

I pay attention to signs daily, and usually see them even if I'm a little distracted.

Just the other day, I was walking Chloe to the vet. I was holding her cone, and had my hands full. She kept stopping on our walk, and I was so focused on her that I wasn't enjoying everything around me.

It's about being fully present. If you have children, grandchildren, nieces, nephews, or friend's kids, try seeing the world through a child's eyes.

They live in their imagination, taking everything in all around them. They often naturally follow their heart and their soul because they aren't in their heads.

Ask Yes and No Questions

When learning to listen to your intuition, ask yes and no questions. For example, *"Is it in my highest good or best interest to go to the gym today? Yes or No"*?

When you ask this question, how do you feel?

Do you feel queasy, get a headache for a moment, feel a feeling of dread?

Do you feel it in your throat, your gut, or your head?

Do you hear or just have a sense of knowing the answer?

Your body will respond in the right way for you.

If you do not get a clear answer and are unsure, you can try each answer out.

Ask the question and say yes. Then pay attention to how your body reacts.

Then say no and pay attention to how your body reacts. I get queasy if it's a no. Over time, I learned to hear the responses. When I first was learning, I would test out both the yes and the no to be sure.

Start with something simple to begin with. Ask, *"Is it in my highest good to have oatmeal this morning for breakfast? Yes or no"*? Then ask, "Is *it in highest good to have pancakes for breakfast, Yes or no"*? Then, you can always do the same thing with which fruit – to eat raspberries or blueberries as a topping. Always start with is it in my highest good or for my best interest. Take whichever one resonates best with you.

When you are comfortable with this first step, next you can ask yes or no by listing various times when she should do something. I love this one for flights, so I always know that I'm on the right airline flight and in the right seat.

If yes, what time? 8 am, 1 pm, 6:30 pm and so on. When you ask the question, see how you feel inside when you say yes.

Now that you know how to ask yes and no questions, let's focus on following your intuition.

Following Your Intuition or Guidance You Receive

This is the action step on your part, where you take that guidance you received and run with it when it's a yes.

If it's a no, surrender, meaning trust that it's not time yet, and that a better opportunity just right for you will present itself.

It's important to remember here that life is always happening for you, not to you.

Everything that you've experienced has prepared you for where you are in this very moment.

It may not make sense, but one day you will watch the pieces all come together when you least expect it.

You have support and guidance all around you.

That's God, Spirit, the Universe, Angels, your inner guidance, or inner compass.

Know that you are never alone, and that so much work is done behind the scenes, so that you can walk forward into a beautiful, blessed life.

I had to take the small, right, aligned action steps in order to walk into my purpose or calling of where I am today. So much of it didn't make sense. It may not be logical as to where you are being guided.

Early on, when I started to follow the guidance or signs all around me in 2022, I was so surprised because they brought me to a local Christian church, and I grew up Catholic.

I also hadn't been to church in years.

Looking back, I had been guided to this church before, but I ignored the signs because they didn't make sense to me. It turned out that I was guided here to help with the Singles Ministry, helping to coach by uplifting people, so that they could see that they were amazing, and deserving of so much love.

Next, I was guided to help coach an eleven- week relationship course. I knew this was the next step, and I started to see the progression. After that, I ran a Facebook group Intuitive Faith and Abundant Living with a few friends where I got to learn, grow, and become a Spiritual Teacher. At the same time, I began to provide both group and one-on-one coaching sessions.

It all started with saying yes to something that didn't make sense to me. If I wasn't open minded, I wouldn't be here today writing this book, teaching a program called Reclaim Your Heart Power: How to Heal Your Heart and Find Personal Power after Narcissistic Abuse.

I would still be in my corporate medical sales job going into hospitals, doing something that wasn't right for me, and not aligned with my purpose.

If you are being pulled in a direction that doesn't make sense, and you keep seeing signs pointing there, maybe it's time to explore it further.

Always do what is right when it comes to your physical safety, but when it comes to getting out of your comfort zone that is a different type of safety that I'm referring to.

It's up to you to know and make a decision as to what is right for you.

Over time, you will learn to grow your intuition.

When you develop more self-confidence, you are being shown the way to what is on your heart.

Be patient, and know it's all about feeling, not thinking, when it comes to your intuition. How does everything make you feel? Following your intuition is meant to lead you to creating the life you desire, to what you are passionate about, and to where and what you should be spending your time on.

Ask yourself these three questions:

1. What do I want to create in my life?
2. What am I passionate about?
3. What do I want to spend more time doing?

What do I want to create in my life?

Envision the life you desire and what you feel in your heart.

Creating a life that you desire is a balance between following the guidance you receive and taking small, right, aligned actions.

You first need to imagine it, and believe for it to come into your physical reality.

Remember this can take time. Follow the steps needed to reach your dreams, which are within reach even if they feel so far away. Keep going and walking forward trusting that everything will happen in the right, divine, timing.

If you recall, I've shared that I've had to take all these small steps, and some giant leaps to get to the point where it was time to write my book, and create my program. I had to grow into, and embody this new identity in order to be living the life I envisioned over a year and a half ago. Be patient with yourself.

What am I passionate about?

Think about what lights you up and what you are doing that excites you, or brings so much joy.

So often these are the areas or things that are tied to your calling or purpose.

Pay attention to what you are drawn to.

Maybe it's a new activity to try or a hobby.

Something you have never done before, but you are curious about. Try new things that pique your interest. Say yes to doing more of what lights you up.

In my case, helping to coach before I actually coached clients was an area I found to be incredibly drawn to, I felt fulfilled, it brought me joy, and it would light me up.

What do I want to spend more time doing?

Ask yourself when you are doing an activity or task of any kind, how does this make me feel?

Ask if you feel energized or drained or somewhere in between? If you feel energized and it sparks joy, then do more of it. Pay attention if you are being guided in that direction. This just might be the way to your calling or purpose.

I was being guided to coach people, and here I was a medical sales rep spending time doing large project management in hospitals.

Then I realized I have been prepared for this, my calling, my entire life, having been guided to work with a number of relationship coaches, a relationship group with women around the country, I often found myself guiding and giving guidance to customers and people I knew over the years.

People were always so comfortable opening up to me and sharing. I guided hospital leadership and the levels in between as well as worked with nurses, step by step through these projects.

I even took a psychology class in college, since I was drawn to it.

I had wanted to major in psychology in college, but my parents thought business would be a better fit, so that's what I did.

Funny how life has a way of bringing you back, or showing you the way to your calling or purpose.

You may not feel ready to think about your calling or purpose. It's not really about that. This is for you to begin to connect with what is in your heart, in other words your dreams. Finding out what interests you, and makes you feel good, will point you in the right direction on your path.

In any case, be patient and get out of your comfort zone by trying new things. You never know who or where they will lead you.

Know that you have the power to set new intentions at any time you want, and to imagine, which will lead to the creation of your dreams in real life. You are not meant to be a spectator. You are meant to hold the paintbrush as you paint with God and or the Universe your beautiful, blessed life.

Authentically You

The more you grow your self-love, self-confidence, and self-worth, it will feel easier to live in your authenticity. You were meant to be seen as the amazing woman that you are.

Continue to show up each day, expressing more of your true essence, letting go of the need to care about what anyone else thinks.

When you are living in your personal power, you are speaking from your heart. You may still have to do things both brave and scared, but the key is that you are showing up. You are living your life trusting that what is meant for you will be for you.

Letting go of the need to chase, you have learned how to attract what you desire just by being you. Having faith and trust that when you truly surrender you get out of your own way bringing so much good and abundance into your life.

You are a woman who sets powerful intentions each day co-creating with God and or the Universe.

Hold the paintbrush, taking responsibility for what you choose to create.

You have discovered that everything is happening for you.

Move forward trusting that you are loved, protected, guided, and supported always.

Your intuition is showing you the way to move you towards your purpose, or calling to live a fulfilling life. You take ownership of what you have created in your current life, and clear out what no longer resonates, as you reclaim your heart power.

You know that by taking the small, right, aligned actions you will move forward to all that is in your heart. You have found that the only love and acceptance you need is your own, and stop looking for that need for validation in others. You are empowered, yet feel at peace, standing in your feminine energy, both creating and receiving your blessings and miracles.

If you hold yourself accountable, continuing to do the work, you can one hundred percent reclaim your heart power.

Walk into your destiny of a beautiful, blessed life.

It won't always be easy on this journey, but you learn to see the blessing or gift in every lesson, the magic all around you.

You'll realize that the power was within you all along miracles will become a part of your lifestyle.

I want to thank each and every one of you for joining me on my journey. Ending this chapter has brought tears to my eyes when I reflect on all that I experienced to get me here today. Everything and everyone I've encountered in my life I see as a gift, an opportunity to learn, to grow, to become a better version of who I was the day before.

It took me so very many years to truly uncover who I was and my life purpose. I feel so grateful for all the tough, painful lessons because they made me stronger, and helped to shape me into who I am today, as well as who I'm becoming.

This book has been a beautiful healing journey for me to release the parts of me that still needed to be freed.

Any one of you can walk forward on your healing journey to reclaim your heart power.

As I said at the beginning of the book, It all starts with you.

Everything you need is already inside of you to create a beautiful, blessed life.

That life will be one that truly lights you up, bringing you so much joy. What's it going to be? The choice is yours.

Reflection Questions and Actions:

1. Now the question is how are you going to move forward from here on out?

2. Which actions will you take?
   Start setting daily intentions with specific actions you can take to make changes in your life.

3. Write down steps you will take starting today to reclaim your heart power.

4. Which parts did you connect most with this book? Pay attention as that may be a good indicator as to where to start for you. This was my path, and that's not to say that you should follow the same order of the steps I took. You are free to pave your own way.

5. What are you passionate about? What excites you and brings you joy? What have you wanted to try that you haven't?

6. How are you going to shift your mindset to see the good in each experience and day?
7. Learn how to control your thoughts. Choose again?
8. What are you going to do to focus more on self-love today?

     ____ Setting boundaries

     ____ Celebrating your wins

     ____ Speaking kindly to yourself

     ____ Self- Care

9. What are you going to do to get out of your comfort zone starting today? What new things will you try?
10. What questions do you still have? Write them down, and feel free to reach out.

It has been a pleasure, and I welcome you to continue the journey with me at reclaimheartpower.com, where you can learn more about my program: Reclaim Your Heart Power.

About the Author

Jennifer is visionary force behind "Reclaim Your Heart Power."

She is a dedicated advocate for women's healing and empowerment after enduring the shadows of narcissistic abuse.

As a bold testament to her unwavering faith and trust in her life's purpose, she fearlessly left behind a corporate medical sales career to heed the profound calling that beckoned her forward.

Jennifer's heart and soul resonate with the profound rewards of guiding women on their journeys to mend their hearts and embrace their personal power. Her journey unfolds in the serene landscapes of Northern California, where she shares her life with her cherished companion, Chloe. Beyond her transformative work, Jennifer is dedicated to self-care. Her passions are evident in her commitment to a consistent fitness regimen, the tranquility of meditation, the soul-stirring melodies of live music, the embrace of nature's serenity, and the simple joy of leisurely walks with Chloe. Her life is a testament to the power of healing, purpose, and the transformative journey towards personal empowerment.

78119459R00072